THE EASTPOINTER

Selected newspaper columns

By

Richard Edward Noble

THE EASTPOINTER

Life in a Sleepy, Little Fishing Village

By
RICHARD EDWARD NOBLE

AWARD WINNING HUMOR COLUMNIST

First Edition

ISBN 978-0-9798085-4-8

Published in the United States of America
by
Noble Publishing, 889 C. C. Land Rd., Eastpoint, Fl. 32328.

Cover, layout and design by
Graphic Designer, Diane Beauvais Dyal

Interior, layout and design by
Carol Noble

Contents

Stories of Franklin County

Franklin County Stories and More

By the Author

My column *The Eastpointer* appears each week in the *Franklin Chronicle*. In 2007 I won the first place award for humor from the Florida Press Association.

Eastpoint is in the Florida Panhandle, across the bridge from Apalachicola to the west and a few miles from the town of Carrabelle to the east. All three of these small communities are located in Franklin County on the Gulf Coast.

In a way this is a history book because the Eastpoint and Franklin County that existed when we arrived are gone. They have not disappeared entirely but they have changed considerably.

Franklin County has been, traditionally, a seafood community. This volume contains a selection of columns that not only present the ideas and opinions of the author but create a portrait of life in the "sleepy, little fishing village" of Eastpoint.

When we first arrived here back in the 80's over 80% of the workers in this county were involved in the seafood industry. We decided to hang around for awhile and live like the "natives." We caught and shucked oysters for our paycheck and fished and crabbed for food.

This book contains an entertaining variety of columns that paint a picture of what Franklin County has been to me and my wife Carol. Most of these columns are light spirited, a few are serious, and hopefully some are downright funny. My goal is that they all contain bits of wit and a trace of wisdom.

In this book you will find stories about catching oysters for a living, operating a small business and living a simple life.

It is my hope that you will enjoy this volume and find it true to my description. Have fun!

Stories of Franklin County

You ain't from around here, are ya?

I suppose that there are a few out there who might incorrectly assume that because a person has lived in the town of Eastpoint for thirty years or so, he could rightfully call himself an "Eastpointer." I am not so naive. I would never, even in my wildest dream tell anyone that I was an Eastpointer. I could no more be an Eastpointer than if captured by a Seminole as a child and held on a reservation for thirty years would I be an Indian.

But when introducing myself to people from far off and distant places like "Tallahassee" for example, I can refer to myself as an "Eastpointer" because what the heck would they know, anyway. They probably wouldn't know an Oysterman from a Fisherman, a Crabber from a Picker, a Shucker from a Culler or a Dealer from a Deck Hand.

Often here in this neighborhood people refer to me as a "Yankee" - sometimes even as a "damn Yankee."

I was informed the very first night that I arrived here in Eastpoint of the difference between the two definitions.

The wife and I were at the old Charlie's Bar when a rather large fellow with a mud stained T-shirt, a baseball cap and a pair of ragged looking, stained white rubber boots came up to the bar next to where we were sitting. He looked me up and down rather curiously and then said, "You ain't from around here, are ya?"

My first thought was how did this guy come to the conclusion that I "wasn't from around here"? I mean it wasn't like I was Chinese or something. I wasn't dressed in a tuxedo or sporting a Gene Autry cowboy shirt and ten gallon, wild west hat. I mean before landing here in Eastpoint, I had been from one corner of this country to another. My wife and I had traveled from Oregon and Washington State to Fort Lauderdale and Key West, Florida; from Baja and San Diego, California to Portland, Maine and Boston, Massachusetts and from the upper

11

peninsula of Michigan to Port Isabel, Texas. Like the song said "We had been everywhere man." And in traveling to all these different places no one ever looked at us and said "You ain't from around here, are ya?" That was weird.

"No I ain't," I said.

"I didn't think so. Where are you from anyway?"

"Well, before we arrived here we were working in Orlando."

"You ain't from Orlando."

"You mean where was I born and raised?"

"Yeah, that's what I mean."

"Well, originally I'm from New England - Massachusetts in particular."

"That is just what I thought! You're a Yankee."

Now I thought that was rather peculiar. All the many years that I lived in New England nobody ever called me a Yankee. I was raised in a town up there that was called the "Immigrant City." We had 40 to 60 different nationalities who had settled there over the generations. I had been called a "Polack" and I had been called a "Harp" and I had sometimes been called a "Limey" depending on which of my immediate ancestors my accuser was familiar with. But no one had ever called me a Yankee.

"What the heck is a Yankee anyway?" I asked.

"Well there's two kinds," he said. "Let me ask you a question. Are you just passing through or are you lookin' to buy a place and settle here?"

"At the moment we ain't planning on settling anywhere," I said. "We plan on staying any place that we can find work."

"Well, we got plenty of that around here. But if you ain't thinking of settling here and you're just planning on passing through that would make you just a plain old Yankee."

"And if I was planning on settling in?"

"Well, in that case, you would be one of them damn Yankees."

Everybody around the bar laughed. When the big gentleman walked away the bartender said "Don't mind him. He don't mean nothin' by it. He kian't help himself ... he's an Eastpointer."

At this point I still don't know if being known as an Eastpointer is a good thing or a bad thing. When my wife and I began our careers as "oyster people" we were working for this fellow who owned a little campground down by the water's edge. We were standing on the "hill" one morning warming our hands over a small fire when I asked the old "salt" if he was originally from Eastpoint. He immediately began laughing and slapping his thighs and elbowing everyone standing around him. "He thinks I'm an Eastpointer," the man said laughing and sputtering. "Can you believe that?"

After the laughing and sputtering died down, I followed up and said, "Well where are you from anyway?" I was sure that he was going to tell me that he was from Georgia or Alabama, or Louisiana or some place like that, but instead he proclaimed, "Why I'm from Carrabelle originally. I don't have no relation to none of these folks over this a way."

So there you go.

My conclusion was that if Carrabelle, 10 miles to the east, was a separate entity to this "Eastpointer" then maybe being a Yankee wasn't all that distant either.

Nationality

"So what nationality are you anyway?" I asked my locally grown little helper over at Hobo's Ice Cream Parlor - a little business over in Carrabelle that I once owned.

"What do you mean?" he asked.

"I mean where were your grandparents born?"

"They were born in Carrabelle."

"Well then, how about your great-grandparents?"

"I don't know, Carrabelle, I guess."

"No. What I'm trying to find out is what nationality you are. You know, like what country in Europe your ancestors came from."

"None of my family has ever been to Europe as far as I know."

"They had to come from someplace. Nobody in America comes from America originally. Even the Indians came from someplace else. Your name sounds to me like it could be Irish or maybe English."

"Listen," the boy said getting a little annoyed. "I'm American, my mother and father are Americans, my parents and great-grandparents are all American as far as I know. I don't even know anybody who's Irish. I wouldn't know an "Irish" if he walked in that door right now. I don't know where the heck you come from but we're all Americans here and that's it!"

I laughed, but it made me think about my old neighborhood. In that neighborhood everybody knew everybody else's nationality. Even today when I talk to an old buddy invariably in our conversation one of us will ask; "Yeah Jack Greco, was he Italian, Syrian, Greek or what?" Here in this community a kid don't know an Irishman from a German. Is that good or bad?

The very next day this old buck walks in the door and starts chattering away. The first thing I notice is that he has a foreign accent.

I ask him, "Where are you from?"

14

He says, "Carrabelle."

Oh no not this again, I say to myself

"No, you didn't get an accent like that from being born in Carrabelle. I know what Carrabelle sounds like and you ain't it."

The man laughed, "No originally I'm from Poland."

"No kidding? I'm Polish too."

"Pardon me?"

"Well, I've never been to Poland but my grandmother on my mother's side was from Poland and her husband was too."

The man stood there staring at me for a long while. Then he smiled and said.

"Let me tell you something. I was born and raised in Poland. I lived there for forty years. Finally I was luckily enough to be allowed to come over here to this country. I know Poland and I know Polish people. You are not Polish."

"I'm not? Well when my grandmother finds this out she is going to be very disappointed."

"I doubt that very much," added the old man. "If I know anything about your grandmother and I think I do, she came over here to become an American. Her children were born here and that makes them Americans. You were born here of American parents and that makes you a double American. Son, take my word on this, you are one hundred percent American. If you leave Carrabelle and travel to any country in the world as soon as you open your mouth those people will know that you are American. You have got American in your blood; it is written all over your face. It is in the way you walk, the way you talk, the way you act, the things you believe. It is your attitude, your style, your manner, your custom - it is everything about you. I know Polish and I know American, believe me you are American. You can not be anything else - even if you want to be. You are American through and through."

After the old man left I began thinking. It was kind of peculiar. I was born and raised in this country but in all of my life living here, no one had ever before called me an American. I have been called a lot of other things but never an American -

15

and certainly never has anyone ever said that I was a one hundred percent American. And when finally someone does call me an American it is a guy with a foreign accent from Poland.

And in addition to all that, unless I was reading this guy wrong, he thought that my being a "one hundred percent American" was a good thing and not a bad one.

I don't know which of those two revelations is the more shocking – that I am a "one hundred percent American" or that someone in this world today thinks that being an American is actually "a good thing."

Thank God for FEMA

If you have lived in Eastpoint any length of time then you have probably met a FEMA representative once or twice. It doesn't seem all that long ago that my wife and I had that pleasure.

It was a very inspiring experience.

A rather difficult hurricane had settled onto our little section of paradise and the wife and I had been affected somewhat adversely.

We had some small damage to our home and a number of trees had been uprooted in our yard. But our biggest problem was that our oyster boat had been wrecked and the Bay was closed down and it wasn't going to open again for some time. Without the Bay, there wasn't a heck of a lot to do around here for work in those days. We had payments on everything. We had a few dollars in the bank but we couldn't stay idle for long.

Word had spread all over town that FEMA was down at the school house and that they had a "plan." Anyone and everyone who was in any kind of trouble were advised to go downtown and talk with the FEMA guy. So my wife and I headed downtown and got in the line. There were hundreds and hundreds of people hanging out and waiting around to see somebody.

We finally got to sit down across from this very nice, smiley-faced guy. He was really quite inspiring. He assured us that all would be well from now on. He asked us questions and every time we told him something pertinent, he gathered up some papers and put them into a folder. By the time we left we had this huge folder about six inches thick. Basically all that we had to do was go home fill out the applications in this folder and send them to the specified addresses and all of our problems were over.

Our understanding was that much of what we had lost would be paid for from some grant programs; what wasn't covered by a grant would be covered by low interest loans from the Federal Government or the Small Business Administration or some other group or program which would be listed in our six inch folder.

This was great! My wife and I left the school house, if not thrilled, very optimistic. In fact, outside of the school house there was stationed a bunch of reporters. One of them ran up to us with a microphone and a camera man on his tail.

"Did you get any satisfaction?" he asked.

"Oh yeah," I said. "It seems that there is a government agency somewhere that will take care of every problem that we have. I lost my oyster boat and the man says that they will buy me a new one; we had damage to our home and they are going to pay to have it fixed; the Bay won't be opened for maybe a year but they say I will be able to get some kind of unemployment compensation even though I am self-employed and have never been able to afford any insurance."

"Wow! So how do you feel about all of that?"

"Well, I can't really believe it. Nothing like this has ever happened to us before. It certainly makes a dim future look a whole lot brighter. This is a great country."

When we got back to "the cabin" and started to read all the information, the "dimness" started to return. The papers were very confusing - in fact we thought that they were unintelligible. We eventually called the FEMA office and told them the difficulty that we were having with all the paper work. He suggested going to a lawyer.

We went to three different lawyers. They all said that they were swamped with applications. One offered to take us on but that there would be a minimum fee of $300 to $500.

We went back home and tried to fill out the applications ourselves - but it was truly beyond our abilities.

So that brings us to our homeowner's insurance and insurance in general.

I am happy to announce that after 25 yrs. of prompt payments with not one claim in all those years, our policy has recently been canceled.

My adjoining neighbors' insurances have also been canceled. When I called my insurance agent about the situation he was not even aware that our policy had been canceled. He said that he would get back to us but I guess he forgot. We went and spoke to him nevertheless. The coverage would now cost 7 to 10 times higher than what we had been paying for the last 20 years or so - if he could find somebody who wanted to insure us.

I suppose I might as well get this all off my chest while I'm groaning here.

Health insurance - I have never, ever had any. I have worked a million jobs all over America, with thousands of people working on all sides of me and they had no health insurance either. I have been in management - no health insurance. I have been self-employed - couldn't afford it.

When I finally sold a small ice cream business that my wife and I had established, the first thing I did was run down to my insurance man to find out about health insurance for my wife and me. To make a long story short because of our "advanced age" and our preexisting conditions it would cost us a minimum of $800 a month to a maximum, with fines, penalties and deductibles, of $1200 a month - if they could find anybody that wanted to take us on and if we could pass the physical. The health insurance companies it seems really weren't looking for people like us.

My wife and I are conservative so we always have a back up plan. If our house blows away, we are going to clear everything off our lot and sell the land, buy a tent and move into the Apalachicola Forest. If either of us gets seriously ill, we have each agreed that the sick one will go off into the woods and die - like the Eskimos used to do in Alaska. The other will report the person missing. If we make it to 65 we have Social Security - I think. I haven't talked to anybody about it. I'm a little nervous. I hope there's not a whole lot of paper work.

19

The river flows or does it?
Move to Atlanta

It was at the Courthouse in Apalachicola over 20 years ago. A group of "politicos" had come to our tiny "fishing village" from the big city of Atlanta - one fancy dressed squirt, in his suit and tie, was from the Georgia governor's office in that land of prosperity and unrestricted growth.

They were here to explain to us why they had the right to take water from the Apalachicola River System for their growing, prosperous, big city in Georgia.

The courthouse was near capacity, packed with white boots, jeans, and baseball caps - no suits and ties.

All the seafood workers knew that Apalachicola Bay needed the river. All of us didn't know exactly why the bay needed the river, but you didn't have to be a real genius to see that there was a connection.

We were all there to learn and the first thing we learned was that as Atlanta grew in size and population, the Apalachicola River level got lower and lower. There was a big lake up there called Lake Lanier and the city of Atlanta was draining water from the river system and storing it in Lake Lanier for drinking water. So the argument was kind of slanted. The suits and ties from Atlanta wanted to know what was more important - the lives of prosperous, hard working, successful citizens up in Atlanta or a few oysters or shrimp down here in this dying "little fishing village" at the bottom of this long river; a village that was filled with dilapidated (rustic) tin shacks and a small group of workers who had the misguided notion that maintaining their subsistence level and traditional livelihoods was being successful,

As the argument progressed our side down here at the mouth of the river was looking shabbier and shabbier. The suits and ties talked about "citizens" and constitutional rights and prosperity and growth, and MONEY. In Atlanta they all made MONEY!

20

The fishermen were all very understanding of growth and prosperity, but they pointed out that this was not exactly an argument of people against "oysters"; it was actually some people against some other people. The people down here in Apalachicola caught the oysters and other seafood, and sold it to other people and made their living. It was people vs. people, not people vs. Polar Bears or Blue Nosed Sap-sucking Yellow Peckered Warblers

The suits and ties understood people needing to make a living but they didn't understand why the seafood workers couldn't just do something else. Like in the Willie Nelson song "don't let your sons grow up to be cowboys, let them be lawyers and doctors and such" - why didn't the seafood workers in Apalachicola just let their children become doctors and lawyers and such and forget about catching oysters and crabs and shrimp.

Here we had the Will Rogers type county-talkin', simple folk in a debate with the Atlanta school of wannabe Harvard graduates with a southern drawl. Talk about living in two different worlds; well here they were.

The suits and ties had flown down here in their space ships and the locals had carted themselves over on their buckboards and the two were here discussing the future.

One group knew exactly what their intentions and goals were and what they were going to do. And the other group was being told to move and make way. And that was it; pure and simple.

Finally one of the white boots and baseball cap crowd said: "Yeah but what about our rights? Ain't we citizens too? I have always heard that this is a country where all men are created equal; where we all have equal rights and freedom. How can you guys just do whatever you want up there and tell us down here to all go to hell?"

"Well, we aren't telling you to go to hell. You're missing the point," said the representative from the Georgia Governor with his wily wannabe Harvard lawyer's smirk. "In fact, if you would like, you could all move to Atlanta too. We'd love to have you all join us up there."

21

The white boot man then said; "So you ain't exactly telling us that we can all go to hell, you are just asking us to all voluntarily move there."

Unfortunately we seem to be getting an instant replay of this past scenario. Only this time it is coming directly from the horse's mouth. Now due to over-development and lack of foresight a new Georgia Governor demands more water for their lawns and putting greens and recommends potential devastation for our commercial and sport fishing paradise. Come on People!

Franklin County business watch

If you are about to open a small business be prepared to meet members of The Franklin County Business Watch.

I don't know if they are a Fraternal Organization, like the Elks or the Moose or the Knights of Columbus, or what, but you can be sure they will be there. They will pop into your business even before you open, just to check you out. They usually make some excuse - like they need to use a bathroom, but what they really want to know is what the hell you are up to, and what makes you so foolish to think that you could ever open anything here in this wilderness that could be successful.

When you finally open your small business, members of this Business Watch will drop in all the time to inform you of the number of cars that are parked at your competition; or to inform you that they were just at your biggest competitor and had a wonderful time and, of course, so did the rest of the community who were ALL there.

They usually try their best to order or buy nothing. Their main goal is to take up as much room as they possibly can. If they get your attention, they will show you their last operation scar, pictures of their grandbaby, their son in uniform or they might want you to go outside and take a look at their new car - or pet ... or new baby gorilla.

Sometimes they just drop in to say hello and give their kids a place to play for an hour or so.

If you sell food, just before they sit down to eat, they will tell you how they recently got food poisoning at the best, most successful eatery in the community, and had to be rushed to Weems Hospital at two o'clock in the morning to have their stomach pumped; after which they usually ask if what they are about to order is fresh or frozen, or prepared today. But usually they just want a large glass of water with lots of ice, and don't be afraid to charge them for it, they advise.

If you do charge them, they will either give you a thousand dollar bill, ask if you'll take a personal check, or run out to their car for an hour, gathering change up off the floor, but all the while remembering to leave someone inside apologizing in a loud voice for not having the money ... TO PAY FOR THE GLASS OF WATER.

They always need desperately something that you don't have: a Band-Aid, aspirin, high-beam headlight bulb, or an emergency room intravenous feeding machine.

"Do you really make any money here?" is a common Business Watch Group question.

Sometimes they will walk in, holding their knee painfully, asking if you have insurance. Other times they just like to stop out in front of your place for a family picnic, or to wash and dry a few of the baby's diapers on your picnic tables or drop off last week's trash in your dumpster.

They love to use your business phone to make hotel reservation in Dallas, or to call back home to find out how Elmer is coming with his chemo.

If you manage to keep the doors open for more than a year and take in more money than you pay out for a month or two, they spread the rumor that you have more money than God and are one of the cheapest S.O.B.'s that was ever born.

If one of your employees falls down or cuts themselves in front of one of them, they usually have a good supply of business cards from personal injury lawyers who they are related to and that just happen to live near-by.

But, let me be the first to wish you the best of luck on your new business idea. By the way, why are you opening a business anyway? Are you just trying to hide some cash from the IRS or do you seriously think that this foolish notion of yours has some kind of remote possibility of being a success? Do you know that one out of every three small businesses in America fail in the first year? That's about the same success rate as marriage. But seriously, is there something wrong with you? Are you incapable of working for other people? Are you too stupid or obstinate to get a real job? Do you hear voices? Don't believe what they say. Take it from me, you are just crazy!

Free turkeys

This is going to be very hard for any of you to believe. I know because it was difficult for me to believe. But according to a book I just read "The Millionaire Next Door," I am in the top 20% of the richest people in America.

At first I was somewhat excited about this estimation but then when I started thinking it over, it really didn't sound all that good for America to me. I mean if I am actually in the top 20% of the richest people in America, this country is in serious trouble.

The fellow who wrote this book is rather old fashioned. He claimed that just because a guy was making $200,000 a year and was driving a BMW that didn't mean that he was wealthy. He claimed that when you subtract what many of the above people owe from what they actually have, many of them are totally broke or operating in the red and getting redder everyday. If they lost their job tomorrow they would lose everything they have.

I am estimated in the top 20% of richest Americans because although I have always been in the bottom 10% of earners and have a poverty income even today, I have a few dollars in the bank, a car that is paid for, a residence that is paid for, combined with no credit card debts or payments on anything. This is, of course, after working for fifty-five years of my life. But that's why I am "rich" and everybody else is poor according to the Millionaire Next Door.

Then a week or so later I stumbled onto this blog about the stock market. This guy who was writing this blog was commenting on an article he had read in the Wall Street Journal where this man who was currently earnings $250,000 per year was complaining that he didn't have any money and that $250,000 wasn't what it used to be in the good old days.

The blogger, who was from a modest, blue collar background, suggested that if his mom and dad had read this guy's griping over his insufficient income they would have very little pity for the gentleman. I was, of course, in complete agreement with the blogger's mom and dad.

Well, then I scrolled down to the "comments" section on this guy's stock market blog.

All of the comments were from people who were earning over $150,000 per year and every one of them was in sympathy with the guy who couldn't get along on his $250,000. They all agreed that incomes over $100,000 per year were nothing to brag about and that they all had to watch their pennies.

I have the strong feeling that while these people may be watching their pennies the dollars are being seriously overlooked.

But okay, that's the prologue to this Canterbury/Eastpointer Tale; now let's go to the real story here this week.

I am standing in front of the meat counter over at the Piggly Wiggly supermarket. It was Thanksgiving time. I was looking at the turkeys. I was trying to decide whether I should buy a ten pounder or a twenty pounder - I enjoy left-over turkey at Thanksgiving time.

Suddenly this lady bumped up next to me. She wasn't the best dressed lady even by my Eastpointer standards. In looking at her I did not presume that she lived in the Plantation gated community for example. Like me she obviously needed some work and possibly a trip to the local Hair Design or Cut. But let's not get judgmental here. Remember those that judge will be judged and none of us really want any of that action.

In any case, she nudges me and whispers; "They are giving away turkeys over at the Such and Such Church. Anyone can get one. You don't have to fill out no papers or nothing."

"Really, why are they doing that?" I asked.

"Just because they're nice people and they like to help folks," she answered.

"Well, that is really good of them isn't it?"

"It sure is. I got one for me - you ought to go over there and get one for yourself."

"Well, thanks for the tip," I said.

Just then my wife came over; "What did that lady want?" she asked.

26

"She told me that they were giving away free turkeys over at some church."

"Really?"

"Yeah, but why do you think that she told me about the free turkeys over at this church? There were lots of other people standing by the meat counter here that she could have confided in? Do I look like I need a free turkey - not that I am above accepting a free anything from anybody?"

My wife looked me up and down. "Well, you didn't shave this morning."

"Yeah, but I'm retired, why do I have to shave every morning?"

"You've got that old shirt on with the mustard stain that won't come out?"

"So? It's my favorite shirt. I like this shirt; it's comfortable."

"You've got those ratty jeans on with the holes in the knees and a pair of white socks with a hole in the big toe with those worn sandals?"

"Are you kidding! I saw a pair of jeans just like these at the Gap, for $147. You have to pay extra for jeans with holes in the knees these days. Expensive socks with holes in the toe will be at the Gap next year. I'm a trend maker here for cryin' out loud."

"Well then don't get all bent out of shape when someone tells you where to go to get a free turkey."

"Who is getting bent out of shape? Where is that church anyway?"

My little yellow marine

We called Sallie's Cat our Yard Guard or our little Yellow Marine. He showed up one day about twelve years ago at my neighbor Sallie's house. Sallie wouldn't adopt the cat so we got stuck with him. We named the cat Sallie's Cat so that our neighbor Sallie would forever feel guilty about her decision. I don't know if it worked but it always makes me feel good — especially when I go out onto the porch and call Sallie's Cat each evening.

All of us cat lovers know that every cat has a personality. Well, Sallie's Cat was a born Marine. He was up at the crack of dawn every morning and screamed and rattled the garbage can until we let him outside. When we let him out, he immediately went on duty guarding the yard and patrolling the perimeter of our "compound." If there were any other cats out there attempting to encroach on our territory Sallie's Cat would confront him nose to nose. He would give any enemy the Marine treatment - ears back, nose forward, very bad look and that Drill Instructor screech.

He was able to dissuade most encroachers but then there was that occasional other Marine who was looking for a fight also. Sallie's Cat, as far as I know, always won but he nevertheless took some licks in the process.

We developed a tough love policy towards Sallie's Cat. We figured that if he wanted to fight all the time then he would just have to lick his own wounds. Oh, we nursed him and did what we could for him but we didn't take him to the vet except as a last resort - a very last resort. The vet is a hundred bucks a throw. I have a rule for all my cats - they get no better treatment than my wife. As you can imagine it is not easy being a cat in my house - ask my wife.

We said; He's a stray cat; we didn't bring him here; he wants to be a Marine; he'll have to deal with the consequences.

Sallie's Cat had any number of serious episodes. He had pieces of his ears nearly bit off; he had infected bites on his paws and legs and shoulders; he had broken teeth and a

28

continuously scraped up, freckled nose - but he lived. He is still here after twelve or more years. My wife and I have really softened to the old boy after all these years. I have personally gained a great respect for him and his belligerent ways.

First, I've come to the conclusion over all these years that he is not a bully - he is just doing what he was born to do. He loves guarding the yard and patrolling the perimeter. He takes no crap from anybody but he loves people so much that on the rare occasion that we take him to the vet he purrs so loud that the vet can't even hear his heart beat with his stethoscope. He will sit in my lap at night and just purr and purr and purr. He is a real lovable, tough, little Marine. I'm real glad that he is on my side of the fence.

But time has been passing and my little yellow Marine is getting older and older. He still goes outside and patrols the yard; and he is still able to scare off most of the regular army but that other occasional Marine is a problem. I've actually had to run outside and rescue my old buddy on one occasion or another. It feels funny having to protect my little Marine after all these years of him protecting me and the wife and all his house mates. I try not to embarrass him. I know how he must feel. I talk to him. I say; "You're doing a good job old buddy. You're still the toughest guy on the block and don't you be ashamed to call for me every once in a while. I've got some responsibility here too. You can't do it all by yourself your whole life and I don't expect you to."

I think that works. I don't think that he is developing a complex or anything or feeling any less of a cat.

Just recently I've noticed that he is getting a little deaf. I think he knows that he has got a problem. He stays pretty much up on the porch and he's always keeping a watch over his shoulder.

A few months back he started losing weight - I mean really losing weight. We had to take him to the vet. He had some kind of a disease that required radiation therapy. He didn't get it. It cost between two and three thousand dollars.

The vet gave us some pills and scheduled us to have some blood tests - for the cat, not me or my wife. The pills cost forty

29

dollars a month and the last blood test was over a hundred bucks. If you count the visit and the basic maintenance the vet bill was over two hundred dollars. The vet cost more than my real doctor. Blood tests and the medications for my cat are more than the same would cost for a human being. This breaks my fundamental rule. My wife doesn't mind taking second place to a cat, she loves the cat too. But as Decider and Chief in this household, I have to draw the line somewhere.

I can't afford to spend this much money on a cat. Something has to be done.

Recently I have been thinking of shooting Sallie's Cat. But I am torn. I love the cat and doesn't he deserve some kind of a veteran's pension for all of these years that he has spent out in the trenches? Do I spend the thousand to fifteen hundred dollars a year to keep Sallie's Cat alive and tell my wife that she will have to do without her cataract operation? For myself I try not to go to the Doctor at all - if I die I die. But, unfortunately, I am the "Decider" in this household.

I haven't decided whether to kill Sallie's Cat or not yet. To be honest I would much rather shoot the vet. I can replace the vet but I can't replace Sallie's Cat. Maybe I could find another vet without shooting the present one but, the way our system works, all the vets are probably about the same. So I can shoot this one or shoot the next one - what difference does it make?

[Attention all Government authorities and Security Police. The above piece is considered to be humor (satire); it is a joke. The author has no intention of killing his cat or his Vet. He has had this cat for 14 yrs. and the same Vet for over 25 yrs. Yes it is true that he loves the cat more than the Vet and that the Vet is ugly and the cat is pretty and has freckles on his nose and many more appealing qualities than the Vet - but Vets have a right to live also – though I think someone should bring this to the Supreme Court to be substantiated.]

Imported seafood - unhealthy

Well, golly gee, I never would have guessed but believe it or not imported seafood may be hazardous to your health - and your kids' health, and your future kids' health, and your kids still in the womb health, and your grandmother's health. Yes, yes the whole family. My, my ... it is so hard to believe. Don't we have government people checking on this stuff?

Ah, actually, no we don't. Less than one percent of imported seafood is inspected in the U.S.

Alabama is one of the few states who check according to an ABC commentary and they reject 50% to 60% of what they see.

Why does it get rejected? Well sometimes the fish is just plain unhealthy; other times it is filled with banned or even poisonous chemicals; sometimes the imported seafood contains banned additives; sometimes it contains chemicals and antibiotics used in aquaculture farming to enhance growth and postpone death in their products that may in the long run have just the opposite effect on you and your longevity; sometimes it contains "malachite green" a fungicide that "studies show" may cause cancer and birth defects; it may be that the fish is actually being raised in raw sewage.

And when the importers get caught using something bad in their aquaculture formula or in their packing and processing techniques, they simply change what they are using and put in a different bad & hazardous thing. And they get away with it because they are confident that the U.S. won't have enough inspectors to catch it. These foreign producers just don't care, says this article from ABC.

But I would like to suggest that today's foreign producer is probably last years American producer who left our shore because he didn't like obeying our rules, regulations, safety requirements, or paying U.S. taxes or wages. So don't think "local" think "global." It may not be "them" it may be "us." It could be YOU!

The world is now filled with conglomerates and multi-nationals. You may be getting a dividend check from some of these "terrible" people right now. Your investment portfolio or retirement package may contain stocks from these very companies operating all over the world exploiting the poor, poisoning the average, destroying the environment, polluting the oceans and ground water and enriching the better-off and the wealthy.

It seems that in today's highly supported and much praised global economy, there may be a glitch or two - like huge domestic unemployment, the loss of high paid skilled jobs, loss of necessary industry, destructive and negative competition, massive pollution, unhealthy imports, dwindling exports and a disintegrating middle class being just a few.

I was reading a biography of George Meany, the labor union boss and he posed a rather interesting question, I thought. He wanted to know if a great nation could survive on an economy where everyone was shining each others shoes. He was making reference to the service industry replacing our once powerful industrial industry. It was once the case that 80% of America's economy was industrial and 20% services. Today it is exactly the reverse. We are in effect shining each others shoes - you remodel my bathroom and I mow your lawn.

A few years back I was investigating this issue of imported seafood. At first I thought the destruction and lack of interest in seafood workers and the seafood industry was a local issue. But then I began getting information from all over the United States. Not just from the Gulf States but from the east coast and the west coast. It seemed that the fishing and seafood industry all over America was on the decline and much of the decline was not due to the local issues entirely but actually the National policy.

It did seem that our Federal and then consequently our State Government because they are attached at the wallet, were not on the domestic fishermen's side in most of these issues. A few dollars did trickle down here and there but it was clear that the big money and the heavy support were going offshore. The foreign fishing lobbies were big business.

And now we see the results - 80% of our seafood is imported and 50 to 60% of it is not healthy or even recommended for eating.

We are told by all the health experts to eat more seafood and 80% is imported and 60% at minimum is contaminated or disease infested.

One of the Alabama fish inspectors is quoted in this ABC article as saying that if it is imported, he wouldn't even eat it - and he would advise other Americans to do the same.

Wow, aren't you glad you live here on pristine Apalachicola Bay? I think I'll buy some nice Gulf shrimp from one of our shrimpers or local dealers or take a walk out on the Eastpoint pier and catch me a few fresh Whiting or Spotted Sea Trout. See you out there.

Annoyance stores

Interestingly enough, I was actually living before the "Supermarket Age." Yes, yes I was actually raised in the "Age of the Corner Store."

The Corner Store had a little bell above the door that rang to wake up the retired old person who lived in a room in the back of the store. Everything in the Corner Store was overpriced - but nobody knew that until the Supermarket came to town. The complaint of the Corner Store owners who went out of business due to the arrival of the Supermarket was that the American people would rather stand in line to save a dime than to support one of their friends and neighbors in that little corner store. Corner store owners were bitter and didn't understand "progress" or "marketing" or supply and demand or technology or economics.

With the arrival of the supermarket the Corner Store vanished - but not for long. Suddenly came the "Convenience Store."

The "Convenience Store" was the corporate version of the Corner Store. The motto of the Convenience Store was "why stand in line to save a dime when you can give us that dime and be on time."

Unfortunately for the general public that dime has turned into a quarter and the quarter into fifty cents and that fifty cents into a dollar.

I went into a Convenience Store the other day. I don't think it was a chain or corporate type but a privately owned version. I was standing in line with my $2.00 wilted green pepper that I had forgotten to buy on my last trip to the supermarket and there was a fellow in front of me with a gallon of milk.

He was obviously a young working man - a laborer. He had the boots and the wardrobe to prove it. He had three one dollar bills in his hand.

The lady behind the cash register rang up the young man's gallon of milk and then announced the price. I think the price was something like $5.35 which seemed considerably more than what milk was selling for at the supermarket. But this was not a supermarket: this was a "Convenience Store."

The young man was somewhat startled by the cashiers announcement, but without a word he dipped back into his wallet and pulled out three more one dollar bills.

As he was standing there waiting for his change he mumbled to no one in particular; "Boy, I'm sure glad I ain't got four young ones at home. Kids need and drink a lot of milk. A workingman could go bankrupt at these prices today."

The lady behind the register said; "Don't worry about them, they have WIC and welfare. The Social Services take good care of them kind of people."

The young man took his change and left the store.

The cashier lady then turned to me and said; "If he can't afford it why don't he just shop some place else - we're not a Discount Store; we're a Convenience Store."

Well, to be honest, I'm in agreement with the young man. I also feel sorry for those young working people who must buy $5.00 a gallon milk for their kids. And young, non-college graduates, working not-so-great jobs in America represent 80% of the younger work force. Interestingly enough many of those who do have good jobs and college degrees are in their late twenties and early thirties and still living at home with good old mom and dad - they can't afford their own home or even an apartment. What is going on here?

Today in America there are 38 million people who, by our American standards, are classified as living in poverty. That's the entire country of Colombia.

There are another 58 million who are classified as nearly poor. These 58 million are living on the edge of "getting by" and falling into poverty. If one of the workers in these nearly poor families loses his or her job or gets sick, they are over the cliff and tumble into poverty.

Thirty-eight million poor and 58 million almost poor - that is 96 million people.

Right now we have almost 1/3 of our nation living in poverty or almost in poverty. During the depression of 1929 we had

35

40% of our nation living in these conditions (though even worse) - but we only had 100 million people in those days.

I think somebody should start being concerned.

I can afford to go to that convenience store to buy a $2.00 wilted green pepper if I choose to - but I'm not going to. That lady turned my convenience into an annoyance. I dislike being annoyed even more that I crave convenience. I won't forget my green peppers at the supermarket in the future and they will no longer see me at the "Annoyance Store."

Fall is here!

Ah yes, once again it is fall. The robins are heading south with all of their little friends. The birds are all a-flutter, the cypress trees are shedding, the grape vine leaves are turning yellow and "I'm as giddy as a kitten up a tree."

Don't you just love fall – everything dying or hiding and going into hibernation. It is just like real life in the world today.

You might think that I have fall fever - if you didn't hear me cursing every morning as I gather up all the broken egg shells, coffee grounds and gooey garbage that had been strewn about my front yard by the raccoons and black bears that are now an integral part of this - the Franklin County Wildlife Preserve.

Yesterday, a little past twilight, as I sat on my screened-in porch, I happened to notice that a fourteen or fifteen hundred pound Black Bear was standing there on my septic tank mound. Naturally I was somewhat apprehensive, so I did what any man would do - I called my wife. She took one look at the bear standing on our septic tank and ran out into the yard to confront the bear. She clapped her hands several times and yelled; shoo, shoo you bad old bear – just like she was talking to the neighbor's cocker spaniel.

I was, of course, still inside the house. I decided that since this was just a big, old, dumb animal in my back yard, I would take some intelligent thoughtful action. "Honey, are you out of your mind!" I screamed.

While my wife continued to play patty-cake with the two thousand pound Black Bear, I called the Florida Fish and Wildlife. I told the man on the phone that there was a bear in my yard. He chuckled.

I said, "What do you suggest I do?"

He said, "Stay indoors until the bear goes away."

I was expecting something a little more than that response.

"Yeah, but what if the bear decides to come inside and join me?"

"Oh wow! That would be something wouldn't it," he said laughing.

"Right now my wife is out in the yard clapping her hands and shoo-ing it."

"Yeah, lots of people have been doing that."

"Is that a good thing to do?"

"I wouldn't say so. I heard about this lady who rubbed peanut butter on her arm and tried to get a Black Bear to lick it off."

"Oh my god!"

"Yeah, she didn't do well. I saw some pictures."

"Well the only weapon I have is a BB gun. Do you think I should shoot it with my BB gun?"

"Oh, don't do that!"

"Why, does that make the bear mad?"

"No, but you could hit the bear in the eye or something and then you might find yourself before the County Judge getting a stiff fine."

"Really?"

"Oh yeah. You hurt the bear and you could be in big trouble."

"Well, what if the bear eats my wife?"

"You shouldn't allow your wife to harass the bear."

"Honey, honey!" I yelled. "The wildlife guy says you should stop harassing the bear."

"But the bear is stepping on my daffodils."

"Yes, but if the bear eats you and then develops heart problems and dies from having too much cholesterol in its arteries, I could be prosecuted, fined or imprisoned or both."

Eventually, my wife chased the bear out of her daffodils, but I sat her down and gave her a good talking to. I said: "You know honey, I took a vow "to death do us part" and it has always been my intention to honor that commitment. Not only that but as the alpha male in this "herd," I have always considered it my responsibility to love and protect you from all harm. But, I must say that if a two thousand pound bear decides to eat you, there really isn't that much I can do about it. Nevertheless, you have my word that I will remove your

38

mangled body from on top of the septic tank - after the bear is gone."

"Thank-you," my wife responded. "You have always been my hero - the wings beneath my feet - I'll cherish your concerns and sentiment."

In any case, if you have a two thousand pound bear in your daffodils, you too can call "the bear guy." He is a lot of fun - not a lot of help - but very funny.

Fish cages off-shore

We were introduced to aquaculture here in Franklin County awhile back. An experiment was conducted here in our sleepy little fishing village and a good deal of controversy resulted.

The experiment was rejected by the County and "leasing" or the privatization of Apalachicola Bay was prohibited by a 3 to 2 vote of the County Commission at that time.

I really don't know what has happened since that time around the State of Florida but recently it was announced at a County Commission meeting that the State of Florida was about to approve another experiment in aquaculture in the Gulf – off-shore aquaculture fish raising cages.

I was covering the County Commission at the time of this announcement and I expected to hear a large outcry. But instead there was virtual silence on the matter from the entire fishing community - local environmentalist and fishermen alike.

This silence prompted me to do a little research and the following is a brief exposure to some of the present controversial issues involved in this matter.

Aquaculture is growing all over the world. Its advocates are claiming it as one solution in feeding the poor of the planet. At its current rate of growth it has been reported that it will only be a matter of time before more fish and other editable seafood products are farmed than are caught at sea. The prestigious NOAA organization is predicting $5 billion in aquaculture production, 600,000 jobs and $2.5 billion in goods and services by the year 2025.

But all of this good news is not without an adequate supply of bad news.

Although aquaculture is being established rapidly in third world countries and touted as a cure for poverty, in reality, it seems to be producing just the opposite.

Struggling poor coastal fishermen are being put out of their traditional work and replaced by armed guards who are hired to protect the shrimp farms at poverty wages. The farm owners are usually from "big business" who are basically exploiting the poor coastal regions with no concern for the natives or their poverty or prosperity.

For the most part shrimp are being grown in these regions for sale to wealthier nations. The native people growing the shrimp can't afford to buy them and the small fish that they once caught for their home markets and local consumption are being monopolized by the Big Farmer Corporations as shrimp food. So now the poor indigenous people are out of work, both traditional and otherwise, and their food has been confiscated as feed for the farms. Once again it seems the rich get richer while the poor get even poorer.

But for those who are willing to accept poverty as an inevitable consequence of prosperity, wealth and growth, there are other negatives to consider. One big negative is the consequence to the natural environment.

The negative environmental impacts from coastal shrimp farming and off-shore intensive fish farming are causing many consumer and environmental groups to ask their supporters not to buy ANY farm raised fish or shrimp.

One of the big problems with the fish farms and cages is the negative impacts on the wild fish population. You may have read about the Alaskan Salmon problem – farm raised fish escape from their cages and bring new diseases to the wild populations which the wild fish are not able to overcome. This same problem applies to the farm raised shrimp also.

There is also a problem with quick growth chemicals and antibiotics used in the intensive farming which add to the other perils already facing the human consumers.

Congested fish raised in cages are polluting the ocean bottom. Fish excretion is high in ammonia, nitrite and nitrate. Overfeeding of the congested fish population fouls the water and pollutes the bottom. Huge areas in Europe where these intensive fish cages are used have miles and miles of sea bottom that is completely dead. The farm shrimp may contain dissolved cobalt and lead - "heavy metal bioaccumulation and lead poisoning in humans is not an exaggeration."

41

If you start reading articles on the Internet concerned with the perils of commercialized seafood farming (privatization of the oceans) you will come upon other familiar terms such as nitrogen enrichment, algal blooms, red tide, genetic pollution of indigenous stocks, decreased oxygen levels, poor water quality, fish diseases, mangrove forest devastation - epizootic ulcerative syndrome and vibriosis with symptoms such as boils, tail rot etc.

If you have any connection with the seafood industry or you are concerned about world hunger and world poverty, the health of the oceans, bays and the food supply in general, you may want to take a look at some of this.

Actually these off-shore fish cages may even be a concern to some of you sport fisherman. I doubt that you will get your prop tied up in one of them but you may find down the road that your Grouper holes are drying up and the few wild fish that you were catching are starting to look and taste rather peculiar.

This essay is, of course, pure speculation and a little trust and faith in your fellow man and the free market system may take care of everything. I mean, who knows? It is all a matter of perspective - is the ocean half polluted or half healthy?

Taking the bite out of your dental bills

Sometimes we conservatives take our innate propensities a little too far.

I have always considered myself a conservative and as everyone knows, conservatives are extremely protective of their money. My personal fascination with money is truly extreme. In fact, sometimes I value my money more than your life itself.

Yes, I am sorry but it is true. For example, if someone says to me; Give me your money or your next door neighbor's life - you're gone my friend.

But that flaw in my character doesn't bother me all that much; most people, both liberals, and conservatives, seem to have that same flaw. What really bothers me is when my love of money turns around and bites me.

I have a neighbor who also considers himself a conservative and he bit himself pretty badly not too long ago. My neighbor is a Snow Bird. Each year his vehicle would suddenly appear next door and I would go wandering over and visit. We would drink some cheap wine and eat some ham and cheese and talk about how dumb the rest of the world was/is.

Well, this one year I go wandering over and there's my good buddy sitting there in his bathrobe watching a Do-wop DVD and eating a bag of marshmallows.

"How's it going?" I say. He gives me a big grin and right off I notice that there is something different about my friend this year.

"What the heck happened to all your teeth?" I shout.

"Oh, it's a long story."

"Well, you can tell me about what happened to your teeth or we can discuss world peace."

"Okay, we might as well stick with reality. I have had this dentist for a number of years now and every year I go for my annual visit. He drills some cavities and fills a few teeth. One day I start thinking and I figure that this guy had filled more of my teeth in the past few years than I have in my head. So I get out all my bills and sure enough this clown has filled like seventy-two of my teeth. I don't have seventy-two teeth.

"So I call him up on the phone and I say; How the heck can you fill seventy-two of my teeth when I've only got thirty-two or thirty-four or something like that?"

"And what did he say?"

"He says bla bla bla, dribble dribble dribble. He gives me this line of trash and I finally hang up on him. So the next day I jump into the van and I head over to this clinic and I have every darn tooth in my head pulled out."

"I see. You don't think that you might have been a little premature?"

"What am I going to do let the guy cheat me for the rest of my life?"

"No ... but how about seeing another dentist?"

"Oh yeah, that's a great idea. You go down to the new guy and first off he's got to take sonar-grams and x-rays of your whole body. Then he's going to tell me that the last guy cheated me and did all my dental work wrong. I'm going to need a whole frontal lobotomy and a rectal dichotomy and twenty thousand dollars later he's refilling all the same teeth that the other clown filled five years ago. You can't win with them people."

"So now you have no teeth?'

"I got plenty of teeth." He reached into his pajama pocket and pulled out a little plastic bag with his new set of uppers and lowers in it.

"Those look real nice," I said. "And how long do you have to keep them in your pocket?"

"I don't have to keep them in my pocket. I can put them in my mouth whenever I want to."

"So?"

"So what?"

"So why have you got them in a plastic bag in your pajama pocket?"

"Well, they hurt like a bugger when I put them in my mouth. It's unbelievable, it feels like there is another person living in there."

"Right ... so ah, let's change the subject. How are the marshmallows?"

"Great, have some? You know I haven't eaten marshmallows in years. When is the last time you've had a marshmallow?"

"Oh, I stopped eating them a while back."

"Why?"

"They made my teeth hurt."

The Wefing's man

I bumped into the Wefing's man the other day at Burger King. I never knew his name, but every oysterman, shrimper, or seafood worker who worked this bay for any length of time in the last forty years in Franklin County will recognize this fellow as I speak about him here in this story. This gentleman worked at Wefing's Marine Hardware in Apalachicola for 37 years. Today he is in his seventies and still looking good, I might add.

I have often wondered to myself if Mr. Wefing really appreciated this fellow. In hobo-ing around America we met a Wefing's man type guy here and there - but his type is rare.

The Wefing's man worked at this store for 37 years. He knew every part number of every bearing, seal, prop or carburetor on every outboard motor manufactured in the last one hundred years. I may be exaggerating slightly but his memory for all these numbers did amaze me.

My wife and I would walk into that store with a greasy outboard motor part in our hand and the Wefing's man would take one look at it and say; "Why that's the bottom bearing on a 1965 Johnson 25 Horse. The part number on that is 933-345-654-975-674397A. I'll go look in the back and see if we have one in stock."

He would return in a few minutes and if you were really lucky he would say; "Well, today is your day. Not only do we have that part but it was ordered in 1967 so you get the 1967 sale price."

"What?"

"Well we mark up the parts for sale in the store when they come in. This part came into this store in 1967 and that's the price that we sell it for today."

"Why do you do that?"

"Why not? We marked it up when it came in and we paid for it when it came in. So why shouldn't we sell it for what we thought it was worth then?"

"Ah, I don't know but it sounds good to me."

On one occasion my wife and I went into Wefing's to buy a block and tackle so that we could hoist our oyster boat up off the ground. We were having trouble getting enough people together to come out to our place in the "boonies" and flip our boat over in our yard. We wanted the block and tackle so that we could hook it up to a tree and then stand our boat up on edge and scrape and paint the bottom. We bought this giant block and tackle that the store stocked in 1946 for $29.35. There were other block and tackles laying around next to the one we bought that were selling for three and four times the price. They had obviously been inventoried in 1956 or 1976. I could never believe this practice, especially when you would walk into the grocery store and every can of peas had six different price stickers on it.

On another occasion we trucked our 1965 Johnson over there in pieces. He took one look at the motor and said: "You got your bottom crankshaft seal on the top."

"How can you tell?" I asked.

"It's easy. I can read the numbers on that seal right there on the top and it's the number of the bottom seal." He then explained to us how to switch everything around. We had bought the motor secondhand. It had the seals on upside down. We followed his instructions and we were back to work the following day.

When I left the Burger King the Wefing's man remarked that I had made his day by remembering him. All the way home to Eastpoint I kept thinking how many times he made my day through the years.

He was always a smiley face, always had time to deal with our problem, he had tons of advice and free instructions - and all at no extra charge. Money was always dear but I always got my money's worth at Wefing's. And that Wefing's man was a big part of that feeling. That's a feeling I don't often get anymore.

If you have a Wefing's man type fellow in your employ, I hope that you recognize him or her and that you realize just how lucky you are. His kind is special. Whatever you're paying him, it's a bargain - believe me.

Captain who?

Now many of you readers out there may not be all that familiar with the nautical and seafaring traditions of this coastal area. For example you might have the notion that a Marine Patrol Officer or a Conservation Man would be a respected position in an area that is for the most part either water or forest. You may even have a relative that has been or is employed in one of these areas. You might even think that to inform a local fisherman that you have a cousin or a brother who works for the Conservation or the Marine Patrol might be a way to endear yourself to a local Eastpointer or a way of making small talk. Well, it isn't.

To tell an oysterman that your brother-in-law also used to work on the water; he was a Marine Patrol would not be considered as a gesture of friendship. It would be like telling a Cherokee Indian that you have a friend who has a valuable collection of scalps and that you could send him some pictures, if he'd like.

So that being said, and if you will keep that in mind, I will go on with my little story.

I was standing on the dock down in Eastpoint after a long hard day of catching oysters. My boss, the oysterman, owner/dealer that I sold my oysters to, came steaming up to the pier in his skiff.

He landed with a bang but didn't punch a hole in his skiff and managed not to crash the entire dock into the Bay. He cut his motor and immediately began screaming. "That Son of a so and so; that no good SOB ..."

"Who you talking about?"

"I'm talking about that no good, lyin', underhanded, good for nothin' Officer Mariner (not his real name). That worthless piece of trash gave me another ticket for undersized oysters. And you know why that illegitimate slime ball became a Marine Patrol in the first place?"

"No why?"

48

"Because he was the laziest, sorriest oysterman this Bay has ever seen. And now I suppose the Marine Patrol Ball is coming up and that useless, lazy no-good needs to drum up some money to pay for his tickets."

"They can't use that fine money for their own personal use, can they?"

"Are you kidding me? Why that whole bunch of thieves have been crooked for so long they couldn't straightened up now even if they wanted to. But I'm going to tell you something; I didn't just sit there and take it this time. I told that sorry bunch of pond scum to get the heck off my boat."

I had been around and working the water long enough to understand most of what my boss was screaming and yelling about but there was one thing that had me a little confused.

The old boy seemed mighty happy and quite pleased with himself for having ordered these Marine Patrol off his boat. This had me somewhat confused. I was not all that familiar with all the "rules" of the sea. I never heard that an oysterman could order a Marine Patrol officer off his boat. But then I didn't really know.

The Marine Patrol Officer always requested permission to come aboard your boat. They would pull up along side our little "Bail A little Sail A little" and holler; "Captain? Requesting permission to come aboard." The first time this happened to me I started looking every which way to find a Captain. You mean we needed a Captain on this wooden bathtub we called an oyster boat? Where the heck was I going to find a Captain? We were lucky we found two life jackets this morning. We dug one of them up off the beach two days before. "Ahoy there! Captain! Requesting permission to come aboard?"

Well, after a bit I got used to that procedure but with regards to my boss and his situation I wondered; If the Marine Patrol must request permission to come aboard, maybe the "Captain" has the right to throw them off. What do I know? Like maybe a man's oyster boat is his castle and they need a search warrant or something?

"You mean you are allowed to order a Marine Patrol off your boat, boss?" I asked.

"Why of course you can order them off your boat. This ain't Russia yet!"

"And he has to do as you say?"

"Heck no! He don't have to do nothing that I say. But I can tell him. I can tell him if I feel like it. I can tell him any dang thing I want to."

"Well, what good does just telling the man do?"

"What good does it do? ... What good does it do? It does a whole lot of good. It stopped me from killing that son of a bee right there and then, didn't it?"

"I suppose."

"You suppose darn right son. You're darn right you suppose."

Help!

I was sitting out on my front porch when I heard a yell. It sounded like a call for help. It was coming from the campground in front of my home. My first thought was that it was just some children playing. But then the voice whined out for a second time. I couldn't imagine why someone would be whining for help in this thriving, peaceful metropolis of Eastpoint but when the voice continued several more times, I decided to put down my book and stroll around to take a look just in case.

I followed the sound of the voice and ended up behind an old trailer where I found an elderly gentleman sitting on the ground. Something had started leaking inside his trailer and he had come to the back of his trailer to shut off the water. He walked with the help of a cane and his cane was laying on the ground beside him. It seems that he had gotten down on one knee to enable himself to reach the cutoff valve and found that he was unable to get himself back up to a standing position. He told me that he had been sitting there for over an hour calling out for help.

I tried to get the man to a standing position, but I couldn't. He was a large man and he had very little strength in his legs. I went knocking on doors in the trailer park to get someone to help me.

The first trailer I tried had an elderly man who had just returned from the hospital himself. He had tubes up his nose and was wheeling an oxygen bottle around with him. The next home had a woman who had just had a knee operation. She was also living by herself and, of course, was unable to assist me. I went to several other trailers. They all were occupied by elderly folks who couldn't possibly help me get a 200 pound man up and onto his feet.

Finally I flagged down an SUV that was passing through the park. I think, at first, they thought that I might be crazy, or maybe that I was a part of a roadside hold-up gang but eventually the man who was driving the vehicle came with me.

51

We were able to get the old buck up onto his feet but it wasn't easy. He had been squatting there behind his trailer so long that his legs were just about useless. We managed to get him over to his front steps. He didn't want us to call an ambulance or anything like that. He just wanted to sit awhile and regain his strength.

In assisting this man I couldn't help thinking about my older sister who is 70 years old and lives by herself on the second floor in a condo in San Diego. She had some bad luck recently and was also using a cane to help her get around.

About a week or so later I was looking up the demographics on this big city I was reading about. The city had a population of 80 thousand and one of the statistics listed in describing this community was that 10% of the population was elderly who lived alone. The city was approximately seven square miles. It had 10,000 people per square mile. It was obviously filled with apartment houses and tenements. So it seems there were 10,000 old people living in tenement house apartments. Many on second and third floors, I would imagine. This was also listed as a poorer inner city community. It had a senior housing development for those with limited funds, but there was a five to seven year waiting list.

One can not help but to think about all those jokes about "I've fallen and I can't get up" or those electric wheelchair commercials where we see all of those old people buzzing around apparently having the time of their lives in their new "freedom" chairs. They seem to be having so much fun, I imagine that some younger people watch the commercial and find themselves yearning to grow old.

One of the disadvantages with being old enough to collect a Social Security check is that you now are old enough to die with everyone's approval. I mean nobody sincerely says, Oh what a shame, and he was only 65 or 71.

Every year old people die from the heat in the summer. In the winter hundreds maybe thousands of old people die because their apartment gets too cold. I've read that on the average it costs $1500 a month to heat a home up north during the winter and we all know the expense of cooling a home here in Florida during a hot spell.

I wonder how many old people are living alone here in the United States? I wonder how many are living alone in trailer parks or on the second floor in a slum tenement house or condo? I wonder how many call out for help and no one comes? I wonder how many fall down and never get up?

Ronald the 'redneck'

Very shortly after I arrived in Eastpoint I met Ronald. Ronald was a very blunt, outspoken individual. He always reminded me of the cartoon character Foghorn Leghorn, the giant rooster. Ronald bellowed and blustered everything he said just like Foghorn Leghorn. You might ask him to repeat what he had just said but it was never because he didn't say it loud enough or with adequate authority.

One of his annoying little habits came with my introduction to his friends or relatives. He would introduce me in the following manner; "This is my friend Richard Noble," and no sooner would his relative or friend grab my hand when he would add, "He's a Yankee."

I would give him my annoyed and frustrated look and when he would look into my eyes and see my anger he would laugh uproariously. He did this each and every time he introduced me to anyone. It was obvious that he thought this to be very funny. I don't know what made him laugh the most, the Yankee part or my annoyed response, but whatever, he just loved it.

Finally the opportunity came for me to introduce Ronald to one of my buddies. I said; "This is my good friend Ronald," and just as Ronald and my buddy went to shake hands, I added, "He's a Redneck."

When Ronald heard someone call him a Redneck, it didn't set any better with him than Yankee suited me.

So from that time forward, as long as Ronald persisted in introducing me as a Yankee, I returned the favor with my Redneck qualifier.

Ronald kind of lived in his own country. In Ronald's America the word freedom took on a whole new curious interpretation. He had a truly interesting perspective with regards to drinking and driving I thought. I'll let him explain:

"Now every man that is worthy to call himself a man has a little drink every now and then. I drink a little myself. Why even Jesus Christ drank a little wine. But I'm more partial to beer myself. Congressmen and Senators, they drink too. Why every other week one of them is found in some motel as drunk as a skunk with some bimbo. Sure, half the time they get it all covered up, but everybody knows. But what really gets me is this drunken drivin' business. My god, what man that's worth his sweat can't drive a pickup truck and drink at the same time? I've been drivin' and drinkin' since I was nine years old out on my daddy's tractor. And what's wrong with it?

"All these pointy heads out there try to tell you that if you drink while you're drivin' your drivin' is "impaired." Impaired my foot! Why I drive even better when I'm drunk than I do when I'm sober."

"Oh come on Ronald, that's impossible."

"Heck it is! I swear, I drive better when I'm drunk than when I'm sober. When a man is sober, he don't hardly pay no attention. I mean there he is going down the road jibber-jabbering, laughin' and talkin'. There he goes with a cup of coffee in one hand and a cheese burger in the other, or smoking a cigarette or something or the other. He ain't paying no dang attention. But when a man is drunk ... why dang it when a man is drunk he knows that he's drunk. He has to pay attention. He has all he can do to keep between them dang lines. And if he don't, why he's over in a ditch before you can say Ty Cobb. I mean if you are drunk and you are trying to stay on some interstate going 70 miles an hour, you'd best be paying attention boy! If you ain't, why you could end up dead with your body wrapped around some dang telephone pole.

"And I'm going to tell you another thing. When I'm drunk as a congressman drivin' home on some dark road in the middle of the night, the last thing that I need is some dufus cop over there hiding behind some billboard. I mean why kain't he sit out there in the open like a man? I mean I'm nervous enough drivin' drunk as a skunk and trying' my best to see where the heck I'm goin' so's I don't kill myself. Why the very last thing I need on top of all of that is some silly, sneakin' cop hiding over there someplace making me more nervous. Don't them dang po'leece know that drivin' drunk makes a man nervous enough and that we sure don't need them sneaking around out there in the woods trying to get us more upset than we already are? If that ain't the dumbest thing them po'leece could ever do!"

"Well, you sure do have a point there Ronald. I guess I never really thought about it in that light."

"No, sure you haven't. Nobody ever does. And that's what's wrong with this country, all the jails are plum full with innocent drunken drivers; they ain't hardly got no room for any real criminals."

"Here here! You know Ronald, you ought to run for the Senate or something."

"You're dang right. I think I should too!"

The Good Samaritan

It was dark outside on the old Escape Road in Eastpoint. We have no streetlights and the road was dirt in those days. I loved living on a dirt road. I used to write to my old city friends back in the big city and tell them that I lived on a dirt road and had a telephone pole in my front yard.

I would often take my cats out for a walk at twilight on my personal dirt road. I wouldn't wear any shoes. I could even wear my pajamas - nobody lived around here back then. It was wonderful to feel the warm sand between your toes - real Tom Sawyer-like. But on this particular evening there was a slight hubbub going on outside. There was a pickup truck on the side of the road in front of my neighbor's home. It got onto the shoulder and it was stuck. I could hear a couple of men mumbling to one another. I figured they were Eastpointers and that they were accustomed to getting stuck and would have themselves freed up in a matter of minutes. But this was not the case. They must have been from Carrabelle or Apalach. It seemed that they were going to be out there forever and I was getting apprehensive about my cat walk. The cats, of course, wouldn't follow me if there were strangers in the neighborhood. So I yelled from my porch to the two men; "You guys got a problem?" One of the men came walking up to the porch and very politely told me that his battery went dead.

Naturally being an Eastpointer, I had all the equipment to jump start anything in the back of my pickup truck. I immediately pulled my truck in front of his and had them jumped in a matter of minutes. They were so happy. They unhooked the cable, hopped into their truck and buzzed off, laughing and waving all the way. I felt good. It always feels good to give a neighbor or even a stranger a helping hand - even if it is just a jump start.

I then took my two little pals, Buddy and Bogie, out for a scamper and a roll in the dirt. We had a good time. They rolled in the dirt, not me.

A day or two later I was talking to my neighbor, Bob. He had lived next door ever since I had moved into the neighborhood. He was a real nice fellow. He was a younger man - only married a couple of years.

"You didn't see anything peculiar going on around here recently, did you?" he asked.

I had to think. What did he mean by peculiar?

"Like what?" I asked.

"Oh you know, like maybe some strangers out here messin' around my place?"

"Well ... no. I didn't see anybody messin' around your place. But there were a couple of guys out in front the other night in a pickup truck."

"Oh really? Could you describe it?"

"Well yeah. It was and older model, camouflage green colored, Chevy - with big tires."

"Oh great, I think I know who it was."

"Friends of yours?"

"Well, not really. They robbed my garage. They stole my deluxe pickup tire rims and some other fancy chrome parts that I had."

"No kidding?"

"I'll tell the Sheriff what you told me and maybe they can get my stuff back."

"Oh wow, I certainly hope so."

After we finished talking, I went back into the house.

"What's the matter with you?" my wife asked. "You look like the cat that just swallowed the canary."

"You know those two guys I jump-started the other night out in front of Bob's place?"

"Yeah."

"They robbed Bob's garage - stole his fancy tire rims and some other stuff."

"Oh my goodness!"

"Yeah, and I helped them do it. I thought that they were rather overly happy as they drove off."

"Did you tell Bob that you helped some kids rob him?"

58

"No. And I ain't going to. I'm just wondering if I can go to jail for being an accessory."

"Oh, of course not ..." she paused. "Well I don't think so anyway. But if I were you, I wouldn't tell Bob or anybody else."

"Oh don't worry, I ain't going to."

And don't any of you out there say anything either. This is just between me and you. Mum's the word. If you squeal on me, and I find out about it - you will be in this column next week - and it won't be pretty.

What about a storm?

As most of us who were around in the "good old days" know, the good old days weren't really all that "good." I was talking with some folks the other evening who had never been seafood workers. They wanted to know what we used to do with our valuable oyster boats when a storm was threatening off shore.

Pictures began to pop into my mind, but the first thing I remembered was that our old oyster boats were not all that valuable. We rented our first oyster boat for a-bag-a-day. We called the boat, bail-a-little sail-a-little. The boat leaked so badly that I had to take a break from tonging every half hour or so, walk to the back of the boat and start bailing it out. Our bail bucket used to be an old Clorox bottle or plastic milk jug with the cap screwed back on and the bottom cut out.

Many oystermen that I knew didn't own an oyster boat or a motor. They rented their boat and motor from the dealer who they worked for - one bag of oysters for the boat and one bag for the motor. Some other oystermen shared one rented boat. Some dealers had a small fleet of old boats and motors that they rented. At one point in our career, my wife and I owned three oyster boats that we rented out to other aspiring self-employed businessmen in the "trade." It was somewhat of a losing proposition. Most of the time, the fellow who rented a boat would get behind on his rent. He would then unload his oysters down on Cat Point or elsewhere and when he came back to tie out the boat, he would have no money to pay.

But the boats were cheap. I think we bought our old boats for between $150 and $250. For most of our career we never had a trailer for any of our oyster boats - and most other folks we knew didn't either.

After many storms we simply joined the large crowd of oystermen who were digging their boats out of the sand along the shore line. At that time there were at least 1500 registered oysterman. The channel in Eastpoint could have five to six hundred boats crammed in that tiny stretch of beach. If you didn't get your motor off your boat in time, you would have to take it apart, get all the salty water out of the carburetor and squirt lots of oil into the cylinder heads, get some new spark plugs and you were back in business again within the week.

If the wind started blowing unexpectedly during the night, I would crawl out of bed, hop in the truck and head down to the shore.

There was a time when there was no breakwater in Eastpoint and every stormy night the shore along highway 98 would be lined with pickup trucks. They would shine their headlights on their boat to make sure another boat hadn't "drug" anchor and was now rubbing up against theirs. If that eventuality did happen, the owner of the endangered boat would have to wade or swim out to his boat, crank it up, move it and re-set his anchors. If it was raining, which was usually the case, and you couldn't afford a battery and an automatic bilge pump, you would have to wade out to your boat and bail it out periodically. Sometime it would get too windy and too rough and all us oystermen would just sit there and count the boats as they went under.

Several times in my own career, I remember wading out to my boat with the wind blowing and the waves crashing, and unscrewing my motor from the stern and carrying my 40 horse Johnson to shore on my shoulder. The boat might go under but at least I would have my motor.

A stormy night in Eastpoint meant glowing headlight beams filled with the sparkle of raindrops, cigarettes flickering behind each steering wheel, and a host of invisible worried, sleepy faces set and determined to face Mother Nature and whatever she had in mind for their future.

When a big storm was announced to be on its way, pickup trucks would be along every bank dragging oyster boats up on the hill as far as they could get them. The trunk of every old car would have the foot of an outboard dangling. Others would be out in the woods hacking down small cypress trees. The cypress trees would be sunk into the mud and used as mooring posts for your old boat if you wanted to take your chances that it wouldn't blow as bad as they said it would.

Digging out your boat after a big storm was a rather strange experience. I remember my wife and me standing on the beach looking at our old boat that had washed up 300 yards from where we had it moored. Old Pappy Millender came up beside us. He looked at our faces. We hadn't said a word.

"Yeah but," he said. "Sure it looks bad now but you'll have it up and running before the week is out and you won't even remember today. What you want to think about today is the beautiful sun peeking up on the horizon on a foggy morning as you're heading out to work, the cool breeze blowing in your face, the clunking of them oysters being tossed into a metal bagging can. What you will remember tomorrow, is all the good times and all the fun that you have had making your living right out there on this beautiful bay with nobody telling you what to do, or how fast you have to move, or when you have to leave, or how hard you have to work. Take my word – you'll forget about today and you will remember the good times and all those good days."

And so it was!

Shucking oysters

"Well, I'll tell y'all," declared the elderly lady ringing up our groceries at the local store. "I was born and raised here in Eastpoint and I've seen a lot of hard times but no matter how hard it got, I never got so bad off that I had to shuck a darn oyster. And I'm mighty proud to say that!"

I didn't know how to take that remark since I had just told the lady that my wife and I would be starting our first day of oyster shucking in the morning. The bay had been closed after a hurricane and we needed some way to get by. How bad a job could shucking oysters be?

Well, let me tell you, it was pretty bad. My wife and I both shucked them oysters as fast as we could and I don't think we earned $25 between the two of us on that first day. An old woman standing next to us had shucked 15 gallons by herself. She complained that the oysters weren't fat. She said she usually did better than only 15 gallons. I remember thinking, resentfully, if she is so good at shucking and makes so much money, why doesn't she have any teeth.

Halfway through the morning we were both suffering from a severe case of "chicken back."

Chicken back is a condition we discovered snipping gizzards and livers in a chicken factory in Arkansas. It is caused by holding your arms and hands up in front of your chest for several hours at a time. We determined that this was an ancient Chinese torture, like thumb screws and getting stretched on "the Rack" or water-boarding.

Oyster shucking involved this very same torture technique. Once that knot tied the ligaments between your shoulder blades in a great big painful ball, there was no getting rid of it. You could twist and shake and jiggle yourself up and down but it would still be there. Imagine someone sticking the tip of a knife into your back one millimeter at a time - all day long!

So half the morning and all that afternoon we suffered through the Chicken Back. Then our legs and feet began to ache and cramp. We noticed that all the other shuckers were standing on a small, portable, wooden platform rather than on the hard concrete floor. We found ourselves two wooden platforms pretty darn quick. It helped a lot.

We were trying to shuck the oysters the old fashioned way - with a hammer and a block. You would bust the bill end of the oyster on a slim metal wedge that rose up from the steel block and then you would dig your knife into the crack of the oyster and pry it apart. It takes more than that to shuck a "pretty" looking oyster but since I doubt that any of you who are reading this will ever be applying for such a position, I'll skip the details. A pretty oyster is an oyster that isn't all hacked up and butchered. It should be whole - with no puncture wounds releasing all the juices.

Once you get the technique of shucking a pretty oyster, then you have to develop speed. When you get good, it appears to the observer that the shucker is popping that oyster from between those two shells with one fluid motion.

It takes a whole lot of oysters in the shell to make one gallon of the shell-less kind. When the oysters are fat (during spawning seasons) you might get one gallon per each bag of approximately 300 oysters. When the oysters are "poor and salty" it could take many, many more. In any case, if you are expecting to make any money don't plan on going home early.

After the first day we didn't have much more money than we did the day before we started - but now we had a plan. The first part of the plan was to get ourselves electric shucking machines.

The basic machine was simple enough and the first one was actually invented by a couple of fellows from Apalach. We went over to this guy's home - as I remember his name was Segree. He and his partner once had an oyster house in Apalach and they supposedly put the first shucking machine together. This old man who was now growing hydroponic tomatoes in his greenhouse, had a number of these shucking machines. We bought two of them for $150 each. I still have one that I use to shuck my oysters when I buy them downtown and we gave the other one to a friend who was going into the shucking business a few years back.

The shucking machine doesn't actually shuck the oyster for you; it simply breaks the bill and replaces the block and hammer. Once you get accustomed to operating the machine, it improves your speed appreciably.

I think the most that I ever shucked in one day was 15 gallons. But after awhile both Carol and I were able to shuck between 10 and 15 gallons a day each. I think the most we ever got paid was $4.50 per gallon.

Both Carol and I have discovered from our careers at hard labor and physical work that when you earn your money by the sweat of your brow, money actually becomes heavier in weight. Sometimes it becomes so heavy one can hardly get it from his/her pocket. It is true! It might have something to do with gravity, the speed of might or air pressure. But I know that it is true.

Retired? What's retired?

So there we were in our lack luster, "no star" campground paradise by the sea, inhabited by all the flotsam and jetsam of the oyster capital of Florida, when this nine million dollar, two mile long wealthy transporter from the planet of the rich and famous comes stumbling down our dirt road, two-track.

Now and again one of these fancy cargo ships lumbered mistakenly down our way in uptown/downtown Eastpoint but usually they took one look around our little oysterman's paradise and slammed it into reverse and were out of sight in a flash.

My wife and I sat there giggling to ourselves.

We watched rather astonished, as did everyone else, as H.G. Oil Wells wheeled his Land Yacht up beside one of the many bent over and half broken electric hook-ups that were scattered here and there about the campground.

After about five or ten minutes, out pops "Dale Evans and Roy Rogers." These two looked like a couple of billion dollars cowboys right out of the fanciest drugstore in America. They were covered with turquoise and what appeared to be random scattered diamonds and rubies. The gentleman had a giant rodeo type belt buckle and his lady was sporting what appeared to be rattlesnake, leather cowboy boots.

"Howdy," old Tex said as he and his bride from Bonanza, or Big Ranch on the Prairie sauntered past.

The lady was carrying something in her arms that looked to me to be a large rat. But this large rat barked like a dog - weird man.

They went walking down by the old oyster shack and then headed off to the right for a walk along the beach.

When they returned there was a crowd of mud daubed, white booted, oyster cullers, shuckers, and catchers meandering around their replica of the QE-2 whispering and sputtering.

The man and his wife stood back and offered the crowd a big smile. "You boys like my little home away from home?"

"Sure enough do," was the majority chant.

"What the heck do you do for a living to be able to afford a dang rig like that?" sputtered one of the Eastpointers.

"Well, I don't do nothing any more."

"Oh you just be one of them rich people?"

"No, not hardly, I worked for the last forty-five years, sweatin' my butt off at a car manufacturing plant up north."

"You worked at the plant or you owned the darn place?"

"No I didn't own it. I just worked there. Henry Ford II owned the place."

"Man! That old Henry Ford must have been a mighty generous boss man."

"Oh no, he wasn't all that generous. We had to fight for every nickel that we got. Henry wasn't giving anything away, let me tell you. We worked!"

"Well, it certainly looks like you got more than nickels. You say you don't work there no more?" asked one old oysterman.

"No, I'm retired now."

"Man that Social Security must be a lot better than I thought it was!"

"Social Security doesn't have all that much to do with it. I get a pension and I always saved my money."

"I tried saving money, but every week when I get done buying what I have to have, and paying on what I can get away with there just ain't nothing left. What the heck is a pension anyway?"

"Well, every month Old Henry sends me a check in the mail."

"What for?"

"Because of all the hard work that I did for him for the last forty-five years."

"You're kidding me? I've been working out on that Factory (the oysterman pointed out towards the Bay) for the last forty-five years and they ain't nobody going to send me no check. And if'n I don't head out tomorrow morning, I won't get nothing to eat tomorrow night."

"Guess you've been working at the wrong factory," the man said with a laugh.

"I guess that I have!"

Turnstile bridge

There are certain people who are particularly concerned with the question – "what's important?" Philosophers, writers, and talk show hosts are a few. As an aspiring "internationally famous writer and author" for most of my teenage and adult life, this has always been one of my particular concerns. Not too many hopeful writers become internationally famous writing about things that really aren't all that important. So every time that a writer takes pen in hand or puts finger to keyboard he must ask himself, "Is writing about the fact that I was born with six toes on my right foot really all that important to the rest of mankind; or is the fact that every time I eat a peanut butter sandwich I get indigestion more gripping?"

Over the years this dilemma has perplexed me for endless hours. But in recent years this problem has disappeared. Now that I have become an "old person" overnight, I have no problem in figuring out what events of my past are important enough to write about. It is relatively easy these days.

I figure that if I can still remember this particular happenstance from my ancient past it must be important. I mean I have already forgotten more than most young people have learned the first thirty years of their life. Actually I consider this to be one of my biggest achievements to date.

Mark Twain once said something to this effect; "My memory has now gotten to the point that the only things I remember for sure are those things that never really happened at all." And I must say I do resemble that remark.

Strangely enough our first day here in Eastpoint and Franklin County is still vivid in my memory's eye.

We came plowing through main street Apalachicola in our Chevy Van towing our Airstream Trailer on Seafood Festival celebration day. That surprise was almost as thrilling as the day we arrived in Mena, Arkansas on the annual celebration day of Lum and Abner.

We were thrilled by all the excitement. We were gawking every which way until we got to the Apalach Bridge. Some contraption like a railroad crossing gate came tumbling down in front of our truck and the middle of the bridge turned sideways. We didn't know what the heck was going on. I now know that type bridge was called a "turnstile" bridge.

We peeked around and watched some of the other vehicles that were backed up behind us. Many of them turned off their ignitions, left their vehicles and began wandering around on the bridge. We decided to do likewise. A few Gulf shrimp trawlers were lined up waiting to pass through the turnstile.

There was a bridge operator sitting in a glass room high up on the bridge and she waved to the shrimp boat captains as they slowly floated through the newly made temporary hole in the bridge. The shrimp boats looked older and even more antiquated than the bridge.

Since Carol and I were hoboes with no particular place to go and no certain time to be there, we just stood on the bridge and watched. It took quite some time for the few shrimp trawlers to get clear of the bridge and on their path out to the Gulf.

Neither of us mentioned it but I know we were both thinking how truly un-American this whole deal was. Can you imagine in New York City or Boston or Chicago if a bridge split open every so many hours and tied up the traffic for fifteen minutes to a half hour? Why my goodness, there would be riots in the streets.

But here in Apalach everyone turned off their ignitions, left their vehicles and stood around on a bridge pointing, gawking, giggling and chit-chatting.

I really didn't know what to make of it. I mean in a world where every day was go-go-go and time was money, here's this bridge that opens up in the middle of the afternoon, stops all the traffic and commuters and most surprising of all - nobody is complaining. They're all acting as if this is an everyday type thing - and, of course, it was. It was hard to believe.

We immediately decided that we had to stay here for a day or two and check this strange community out. There may have been other places with bridges like this but in all our travels we never saw another.

We found a little campground right on the water for $25 a week rent and then we ran over to another bridge and fished off the 'catwalk' - not too many places had catwalks either. We caught the biggest flounder that I had ever caught in my life and a great big red fish.

It was a memorable day. And now 25 to 30 years have passed and we are still here. To be honest there has not been a week that has gone by in all this time that I haven't thought of hitting the open road once again but yet I haven't. Someone once said to me that once you get some of that Eastpoint sand in your shoes, you just can't get rid of it. So far that seems to be the case.

Dottie the dumpster diver

Dottie lived in Eastpoint for a number of years. We don't know exactly when she got into Dumpster Diving but she developed a serious addiction.

If you have never done any Dumpster Diving yourself you wouldn't really understand.

My older brother became a chemist and he worked for a guy who owned a smelting plant. The man who owned the plant where my brother worked was the son of a ragman. Kirk Douglas wrote a book entitled The Ragman's Son. But my brother's boss was really a sophisticated ragman. Professional ragmen and scavengers of all types brought their collected radiators and bicycles and water heaters and copper wire to the plant where my brother was employed. My brother supervised the smelting process and turned the scrap metal into ingots that his boss sold to somebody. The ragman's son who my brother worked for was a multi-millionaire.

Carol and I did a little Dumpster Diving when we were out in California Hobo-ing the U.S.A. We dove into the dumpsters looking for aluminum cans that we crushed and stored in a canoe that we had anchored to a rack on top of our van camper. We gave it up when we noticed that we had our own colony of flies following our camper wherever we went. We were like that kid in the comic strip that had a dark cloud hovering over his head.

But Dottie was retired and she started Dumpster Diving for aluminum cans and a few extra pennies originally. After a few "dips" she found, just as Carol and I discovered, dumpsters had all sorts of good stuff in there - especially if you go to dumpsters in better neighborhoods. It is amazing what some folks throw away. We sometimes found brand new items that had been stuffed back into their original boxes just because the person who had bought the item couldn't figure out how to put it together. It was amazing and somewhat shocking.

Every time we drove by a dumpster we would see Dottie's car parked beside it and Dottie's head bobbing up and down from inside the dumpster. She had a nice new car. She wasn't really a poor person.

It wasn't long before Dottie had ventured out into distant lands. First we saw her in Port St. Joe, then in Panama City. We saw her in neighborhood dumpsters and behind shopping malls. Her whole appearance began to change. Gradually her wardrobe got shabbier and shabbier. She bought some white rubber boots like the fishermen and oystermen wore. She had a knit cap pulled down over the top of her head like the boys in the hood. She wore a long overcoat. Her complexion got darker or maybe it was dustier. Her whole personality changed. Needless to say she no longer had her nails and hair done on a regular basis. She had a little Toy Poodle. It was white ... then off white ... then a dusty gray. It was something to see how dumpster addiction could affect the whole family.

Dottie became rather detached. She stopped talking to people ... well maybe people stopped talking to her. She was always carrying black garbage bags in and out of her house. Very soon she had them stacked up against the outside walls of her trailer.

The neighbors were affected also. Every time a neighbor came home they stood staring over at Dottie's place for several minutes. Finally they would shake their heads and go inside.

Dottie went from diving to collecting. Dottie had always been a thrifty, penurious type individual and when she stumbled onto this parking lot gold mine, she got the habit. Dottie now had a "dumpster on her back." She couldn't resist picking up anything of value, even if she didn't know what to do with it.

We would visit her occasionally and we noticed that her doublewide was getting smaller and smaller - and harder to find. First she filled the spare bedroom; then her bedroom; then she started stacking boxes along the walls; then out on the screened-in porch; pretty soon you could barely get up to or into the house.

She started filling her yard with storage sheds. She had her own yard sale business. We never went because ... well we knew her "suppliers." There was also a rather distinctive odor emanating from the area.

One day Dottie just disappeared. We don't know what happened to her. Her lot was cleaned up and her doublewide was replaced. Our guess was that Dottie was finally called to that big dumpster in the sky where one person's trash is another person's treasure and the streets are lined with dumpsters of gold.

Garbage had become Dottie's life but unlike the Ragman's Son Dottie never learned how to market her garbage. There is a moral to this story somewhere but I guess you will have to find it for yourself. I have no clue.

Oyster theory of value

It was a horrid day in Paradise when either my wife or I asked the question, "Do you realize how many bags of oysters this is costing us?"

I don't remember which of us thought it up but from that day forward, spending our money became a rather frightening experience. Neither of us had ever made such an analogy before in our working careers. Never before had we equated our work to our purchases and bills. How many dishes did I have to wash to pay the light bill or how many chickens did I have to cut to run the air-conditioner? Once we got onto the oyster bag standard of value everything suddenly became far too expensive.

When we started our oystering career we sold a bag of oysters for $4.00. Consequently it didn't take a very large purchase to amount to a substantial number of bags of oysters. A pizza and a pitcher of beer could be 5 or 6 bags of oysters. A special dinner or a night on the town could easily turn into ten or twelve bags of oysters. That could be a whole day's work for the two of us depending on the time of year.

The big problem was imagining carrying 5 or 6 bags of oysters up to the counter at the local pizza joint. Why in the world would we be willing to trade 75 to 80 oyster dinners for one pizza and a pitcher of beer? Were we Crazy?

We did a lot of staying at home and eating fried oysters and fresh caught fish instead of T-bone steak or even fried chicken. I would often help load a truck down at the oyster house for 25 or 30 stone crab claws. I thought that was a great deal - 2 or 3 hours of work for 3 or 4 stone crab dinners for two. My wife really liked that trade - especially since it involved my labor only.

If a hamburger and a beer cost 5 dollars and a bag of oysters was selling for $4.00 that was a very poor trade. Do you know how many oyster burgers a person could make out of one bag of oysters? If you figured six fried oysters to the bun, that would be about 50 oyster burgers to the bag. Why would anybody trade 50 oyster burgers for one hamburger?

We were off the dollar standard and the gold standard. We were now on the bag-of-oysters standard. Do you know how many bags of oysters it took to buy a washing machine or a new mattress? A new automobile took the oyster bag standard off the charts.

Then a strange thing happened. The price of oysters began to climb. The rules had changed and consequently we were able to catch fewer bags, but nevertheless we made more money.

A bag of oysters at one point was selling for as high as $20. Now from the sale of just one bag of oysters we could buy 4 T-bone steaks at the grocery store or one pizza and a pitcher of beer at the local restaurant. One bag of oysters could buy 10 or 12 pounds of hamburger. We could go to a movie in Tallahassee and even buy a bag of popcorn for one bag of oysters. Ten or fifteen bags of oysters could buy a new washing machine or a stove. We were fortunate to be in a period where the price of oysters rose faster than the price of everything else. That, of course, has since changed.

But then we had a different problem - would we rather eat fried oysters all week or T-bone steak and hamburgers? At $20 a bag of oysters we really couldn't afford to eat oysters any more. We stopped taking oysters home altogether. Just a quarter of a bag of oysters could buy a pound of hamburger and a six pack of beer.

We were now pulling up the floor boards on our boat to make sure no oysters fell through the cracks. I remember telling Carol one afternoon, "I feel like eating oysters tonight and I don't care how much they are costing us." We rebelled against the economic system that evening and ate a whole pail full of steamed oysters and a full plate of fried oysters. That one dinner may have cost us 10 pounds of hamburger and two six packs of Bud. Talk about going crazy! What was it with us? Did we now have bags of oysters to burn?

It seemed totally insane. We were the people who caught the oysters. The oysters always cost us so many hours of sweat no matter what the price. But now because of some external standard of value - we felt that we could not afford to eat our own oysters any more. What is that?

Actually I can't afford to live here in Eastpoint anymore. Not too long ago they were telling me that my pink single-wide situated in the middle of a one acre swamp was worth $200,000 to some guy living in London or Paris, France. Does anyone out there have that man's phone number?

Countywide vs. single district voting

This is a difficult issue to understand and I still don't know if I have it down accurately. Somebody will have to contact an expert on Civil Rights legislation and voting rights. But nevertheless I have been trying to bone up on this issue and come to an understanding of it.

The following is how I understand this issue after limited studying of the legal jargon involved.

The first areas of contention are the principles of majority rule and minority rights. This confrontation goes back well before the establishment of the United States. This is a problem intrinsic to the political concept of democracy.

That the "majority" should rule has always been problematic. Philosophers have long warned against a possible "Dictatorship of the Majority" in democratic structures. Our whole structure of government is designed to counter just that. We have two representative bodies; one regulated by population and the other by simple membership. The House is population (majority) and the Senate is simple membership regardless of population - there are two senators form each state no matter what the size or population of the state.

A Bill of Rights was also established by the smaller states to protect their minority status, and the ninth amendment to protect us from our own Constitution. The ninth amendment reminds the populace that we retain rights NOT listed in the document. That we have RIGHTS other than those listed is the basis for much of the arguments related to the Supreme Court today.

In the 1960's it was decided by the Supreme Court that certain minorities were not being provided a fair representation in the governing of this nation. Changes to guarantee fair representation to these minorities were written into the law of the land. As a result of this legislation in 1963, twenty years later, in Franklin County, Florida, a legal action was taken to the Florida courts claiming that the traditional voting practices in Franklin County were not adequate to provide fair representation to all of its constituents.

The traditional practice of countywide voting was challenged by the local black community. This challenge was at the financial expense of the black community. They received no help or funding from the local government or the County Commission as far as I know.

In their case they brought in historical documentation stating that the practice of countywide voting was not adequate, was biased and prejudicial and made it impossible for blacks in Franklin County to be represented. The court decided in favor of the black community and placed an "injunction" against Franklin County and the practice of countywide voting.

This decision mandated that Franklin County devise a new system of voting that would guarantee a fair representation to the black community.

There were several different methods of voting that were accepted and approved as democratic that could have been enacted but the single district was decided upon as being the simplest, least confusing and least disruptive.

Since it was the winner-take-all, countywide, majority rule voting practice that was declared in violation of the law, the majority community cannot simply have a majority countywide voting referendum to overrule this legal action. It is the majority rule voting that was declared illegal in the first place.

A legal case must be taken to the court on behalf of those who are challenging the decision to override that decision.

My estimate is that the group that would like to pursue this action will have to have a very good team of lawyers with stacks of recent historical documentation and lots of money. I don't think that the County has enough taxpayers or taxpaying citizens to want to pursue this controversial expense. To ask the local County Commission to support one side or another in this action would be asking the commissioners to act "undemocratically" not democratically and to champion racial

78

bias. It has already been stated by prominent members of the black community that they will make a legal challenge to any such action challenging their right to political representation in this County.

The winner take all countywide policy is still being challenged on other grounds all over the United States. Many communities even without a black constituency find this practice unfair and challenge it simply on the basis of its potential to empower a strong voting block of just 51% of the registered voters. With this system there is the potential that a small but well organized block of voters could take over any local government.

This is a big concern in areas where development is a prominent issue. Those who have enough money and backing could unfairly dominate the voting population and force this issue to one outcome or the other.

In summary, I do not think that the voters of Franklin County have the option of going back to countywide voting even if a majority of the voting population would like it better that way. Just as the majority of citizens in the entire nation as a whole could not vote slavery back into law even if they thought it advantageous or better suited to the needs of the majority.

In the United States of America the majority doesn't necessarily rule and it never has. The rights of minorities and individuals have always been a huge concern of the American people.

Hurricane evacuations

A while back when I was covering the county commission meetings, an elderly woman from Apalachicola stood up and attempted to explain to all the listeners why it was that folks who work in the seafood industry are reluctant to leave town even when a hurricane is approaching. My wife and I have been two of those people.

We weathered most of the storms that struck in this area in our little mobile home. We slept on the floor over at Hobo's Ice Cream Parlor, when we owned it during one storm. We hauled our mattress from home and a bunch of blankets. My wife even had her favorite pillow. It blew pretty hard and it was mighty scary. We didn't sleep much that evening – even with our favorite pillows.

To be very honest for the most part we never left because we didn't have the money. Even twenty years ago, it cost fifty or sixty dollars to stay in a motel. We had no friends or relatives in the area we could visit. It didn't make much sense to us to be up in some forest or parked sleeping in our car north of Eastpoint in a hurricane. So we took our chances and sat it out. I have no difficulty associating with those "po" folks in Mississippi and hurricane Katrina. In our day we would have been right up on that bridge with the rest of them.

We left during only one storm. They were predicting over 150 mile an hour winds. Our new friend Ronald the Redneck had invited us up to his place in northern Florida if it ever got bad. So we gave old Ronald a call and he said, "Sure, come on up!"

I think Ronald made the offer in the spirit of generosity but was surprised when we took him up on it. But surprise or no surprise we got the royal treatment up at Ronald's place. He took us all over town. We met all his friends and relatives. We even went over to a buddy of his and watched them make cane syrup. Ronald's wife was one of the best home cooks I have ever met. I had food that I never experienced before - like

80

deep-fried corn bread and chicken fried steak and gravy. I'll never forget it.

The hurricane landed and we watched it on TV every chance we got. I remember Ronald being curious about our concerns. He had a nice home and lots of possessions. He was aware that we lived in an old Airstream travel trailer parked on our lot on a bed of oyster shells with a septic, a light pole and our oyster boat out back - that was it. Finally he said, "You folks are so worried and you really don't have all that much to lose."

I said, "It may not seem like much to you, but it is all we got to us."

I know Ronald liked that answer because from then on that is what he told any of his neighbors who asked what we were doing up there. "They are running away from that hurricane. They don't know yet but they may have lost all they got." Most of his neighbors were impressed by that remark because they knew how devastated they would be if they lost "all they got." None of them knew how little all we had was.

One of the most interesting things about being away during a hurricane was watching the news. The news reporters, understandably, go to a spot that looks the most devastated to them and they start filming. "And here we are out in front of this devastated building. As you can plainly see the hurricane has taken its toll."

The trouble with that scenario in our case was that most of Eastpoint looked like a hurricane had struck it before any hurricane ever landed. The news media was on the Eastpoint waterfront taking pictures of the dilapidated oyster houses that had been dilapidated for the last 50 years. They were constructed dilapidated. They were built by Dilapidation Construction Inc.

My wife and I kept staring at the TV trying to figure out where the devastation was. We saw on TV the dealer house that we sold our oysters to and the only difference was the depth of the water and the waves crashing over the rickedy dock. There was nothing damaged at all as far as we could see. In fact after that storm, all the Dealers collected their insurance money and the shoreline in Eastpoint got a face lift. It had never looked so good before in its entire history. I wondered at that time, why they built such nice expensive buildings right along the water's edge. The dumple-down old oyster shacks and rickety unloading docks made more sense to me. Our recent hurricane Dennis I think has reaffirmed my contention.

I know this does not conform to "conventional" wisdom but if you are going to build your house on a railroad track, cheap and shoddy might be just what the doctor ordered.

No pizza in Franklin County

When we first arrived here you could not buy a pizza in the entire Franklin County - no pizza house, east or west. The first Pizza Parlor to open up here was Risa's Pizza in Apalachicola. It was opened by a nice fellow and his wife from Port St. Joe. He had worked for one of the mills in St. Joe for a number of years and was laid off.

Not too long after Risa's opened, BJ's opened up out on the Island. They both sold a good pizza but most of us Eastpointers went over to Risa's because it cost two dollars to get over the St. George Island Toll Bridge. Two dollars, man! Can you believe it?

Carol and I went out to the Island maybe once a month as a kind of adventure. There wasn't really all that much out there. The biggest attraction for us was a place called the Dingy. It had a real Island atmosphere. All you had to do was sit down at the little bar and you were in the middle of a conversation. The Dingy was mostly working people while Harry A's had a more sophisticated reputation. Of course, sophisticated in Franklin County was a rather tenuous thing.

Other than some construction jobs and some fancy homes, the Island had very little to offer. There was a parking lot at the east end and you could walk or drive down to the cut on the west end, if you chose to.

Apalachicola was worse - it was a ghost town. The main street on both sides of highway 98 looked like it was permanently ready for the next hurricane — many of the windows were boarded up. Everything was closed down and empty.

If you wanted a hamburger you could go east or west from the Hub of Eastpoint. We almost always went to Johnny's over in Carrabelle.

Johnny's was on the water side of 98 in Carrabelle in a modest building. Everybody was friendly over there - unlike the Grill over in Apalach. The Grill before the new folks took it over was a rather strange experience for "foreigners" like us.

When you walked into the place there was a big round table to the rear on the left side if your back was to 98. At this table "lived" a community of ten or so older looking men. They were always there. I really don't know what they were doing there. We figured that they were the homeless relatives of the owner.

They never seemed to be eating anything. They all drank coffee. On one occasion I was rather surprised to overhear one of them request an order of toast. They had to wake the cook up to make it.

No matter who walked in the door, this whole table turned around and stared at them. As a potential customer one couldn't help but have the feeling that you were under suspicion. We felt so icky going in there that we avoided the opportunity whenever possible.

Today's Grill is one of the busiest restaurants in Franklin County. And the new owners are very friendly – in fact, I once worked there. They boast serving the largest fish sandwich in the world – and I was there when they devised that idea.

There was no place to eat in Eastpoint until Mom opened up. Mom's was unique. It was located where the pawn shop is now. If there were more than two cars parked out front, you might just as well skip breakfast.

Mom had a problem with organization. First you would get your eggs - but now your coffee cup was empty. As Mom put down your eggs, she apologized for the toast and would promise you another cup of coffee as soon as it was ready. She would then go and get it ready. Then came the grits. Mom would, of course, have to run and get you some butter. The butter would sit on top of the grits like a polar bear on an iceberg. When the toast came, Mom would agree to put your grits in the microwave. Mom would remember your grits at just about the time you were standing at the cash register to pay your bill. Breakfast was always an experience at Mom's. Everybody loved her - she tried so hard.

On that rare occasion that we went out to eat and bought something more expensive than a hamburger and French fries or a breakfast of grits toast and eggs for 99 cents, we went out to the lodge - not the prosperous Bay City Lodge that is owned by Jimmy Mosconis (which is great!) but the Breakaway Lodge that is now gone as far as I know.

I never bumped into a fellow oysterman at a restaurant until Sharon's opened up in Eastpoint a few years back. It is now gone also. Despite rumors to the contrary most oystermen didn't make enough money to be eating dinner out at a sit-down restaurant.

The Gibson Inn was condemned when we first arrived. They were going to tear it down. I understand that is the reason Mr. Ben Watkins bought the old hotel. He then found some investors who, with the help of a State historical grant, turned the abandoned building into a tourist destination. I actually feel the remodeling of the Gibson Hotel was the turning point towards prosperity here in Franklin County.

The Gibson attracted a whole new group of investors and entrepreneurs who started buying and remodeling all of Apalachicola - and from there things seemed to snowball into the thriving Goliath that we enjoy today.

Living in a trailer home

"I don't think that they should allow people to live in those trailer homes."

My sister, calling me from San Diego, California, said that to me the other night on the phone. And she knows all too well that I have lived in my trailer home for over 30 years now. Sometimes it is hard to believe what a family member will say.

I didn't get angry or even annoyed; I decided to practice my Socratic Dialogue techniques.

"And why do you say that, my dear sister?" I inquired Plato-like.

"Well, you know why! Every time there is a storm somewhere they show some trailer park in a shambles. It's ridiculous! Those trailer homes aren't safe to live in."

"Well, I've been living in a trailer home for thirty years now and I'm still here."

"You've been lucky."

"I've been lucky? And this is coming from a person who lives in California, the land of mud slides, earthquakes, forest fires and collapsing bridges? As I remember last year, you had a fire that surrounded your entire area. You told me that you had to evacuate your condo. I couldn't contact you for three days."

"Well ..."

"Well what? Because you were living in a condo you were safer from the surrounding flames than you would have been if you were living in a trailer home?"

"No, I guess not"

"And if it had been an earthquake you would have been safer in your fancy condo than in a trailer home?"

"No."

"And it is safer to be in a condo during a mud slide?"

"No, but what about a hurricane?"

"Well, there is plenty of warning that is given when a hurricane comes. We've always had plenty of time to leave the area if we felt endangered. We've had several hurricanes come through here and we're still here and so is our trailer home."

"But what about a tornado?"

"Do you think that a person is safer in a conventional home than he is in a trailer home in the event of a tornado? A tornado doesn't care if something is made of cement, brick, plastic or steel - a tornado will rip anything apart and it doesn't come with a week or two of warning advisories."

"I know. But when all those trailer houses get destroyed, it cost those insurance companies millions of dollars. They don't even want to insure trailer homes anymore."

"You're right. But I don't think it is because the insurance companies are worried about saving lives. I think that it is because they would like nothing better than to see all the trailer homes disappear so they could be replaced by million dollar apartment structures like yours, or a pile of fancy homes paying them big premiums like out on St. George Island. You know the last close call we had here in Franklin County, our trailer home was still in tact. Our only damage was to the screens on our porch. St. George Island was a wreck. My wife and I went out there with our boat trailer and gathered up enough building supplies laying out on the roads to build two out-building here on our property. We paid trailer insurance for over 20 years and never made a single claim.

"When there is a storm and the insurance companies pay out millions - most of that money goes to home owners not trailer parks. To replace the cost of one 3 million dollar home out on the St. George Island every trailer in Eastpoint would have to get blown away. The reason insurance companies don't want to insure trailers is the same reason they don't want to insure sick people - they can't make any money off the poor and the sick. They're a business! Businesses want to make money - they aren't the United Fund, Red Cross or the Salvation Army you know."

"I know. But that is the way it is."

"Well, let me tell you something else. If it were just safety and cost, they wouldn't allow anybody to live in anything but a trailer or some other cheap expendable type living structure around here and the water's edge. If it was just a matter of safety and cost, they wouldn't let anybody build an expensive home on a barrier island or along a coastal area. It wouldn't matter if it was elevated up on stilts or not. It is all a matter of premiums and profits - not people, safety, and costs. Sure a trailer home can blow away but if they kept them cheap and affordable they could be insured for a small cost and replaced when and if a few of them get blown away every twenty or thirty years."

"Well, how come they kept telling us on the news about the danger of these cheap trailers?"

"Who do you think owns the TV stations - trailer park operators or insurance companies and big investors? My dear sister, if it weren't for this trailer home Carol and I would never have had any home. It isn't the most beautiful home on the block even in Eastpoint, but we have had a good life here and a lot of fun playing house in this cheap little pile of tin. Now the insurance companies want to charge us $3,000 a year to insure a $10,000 trailer. They don't want to help us; they want to get rid of us!"

Harvester of the sea

If you have lived in Franklin County for any length of time, you have probably heard a seafood worker compare his life to that of a farmer. The first time that I heard such a comparison, I smiled, thinking it to be, more or less, a joke or another example of misplaced logic.

But over the years of working as a seafood worker, I began to feel some of that spirit myself.

Many oystermen, shrimpers, crabbers and fishermen will refer to what they do for a living as "a way of life." That is a phrase that I have often heard farmers use - maybe you have also.

Seafood workers look at Mother Nature as a business partner. Mother Nature can be a rather difficult boss sometimes but overall, she makes the rules and provides the income. I have never seen a seafood worker complain about the demands put upon him because of the perils of Mother Nature. Farmers have pretty much the same attitude.

Seafood workers are oftentimes more environmentally conscious than farmers. Seafood workers deal with Mother Nature in the raw - no pesticides, no sprays, no fertilizers and not too many sophisticated adaptations benefit their industry.

When they came to Franklin County with the modern farming techniques of aquaculture, it was rejected primarily because of its "unnaturalness."

I was always amazed at how the seafood workers responded to natural tragedy. They never seemed to get upset. They always wanted to go back to work as soon as possible. If they had a boat wrecked, they patched it; if a motor failed or went under they cleaned and fixed it. They seemed a rather unflappable group - rather old-fashioned and ever convinced of the "old ways."

So it especially interested me the other day when I read an article about a 1962 Nobel Prize winning economist, Amarta Sen, who discovered that there was an inverse relationship between the size of farms and the amount of crops they produced per hectare. It seems that the smaller the farm the greater the yield. And recent more in-depth studies are confirming Sen's research.

This notion is contrary to conventional wisdom - and contrary to the wishes of Agri-bis Inc.

I remember discussing this years ago here in Franklin County. I suggested in a letter to the editor that the old fashioned tonging method of harvesting oysters may actually be more productive, more efficient and of more social benefit than dredge or machine harvesting. My notion was that in some cases small, inefficient and even primitive might actually be better in the long run than big, efficient and mechanized.

It is difficult to believe that some guy with an ox and a handmade plow can out produce an Agri-bis international conglomerate on a per hectare basis but studies in Turkey, India, Pakistan, Nepal, Malaysia, Thailand, Java, the Philippines, Brazil, Columbia and Paraguay stand testament to the notion. Land reform in Japan and South Korea, where large farms were broken up after World War II and divided among small farmers, have been said to be an economic miracle - and a similar result is said to be happening in China. The opposite is the case in the U.S. and Western Europe - the big are growing while the small are disappearing.

I also remember reading about the "unexplainable" circumstance that was taking place in Communist Russia a few years back. The Russian peasants were given the right to grow their own personal vegetable gardens in their free time away from their full-time jobs on the big collective state run farms. It seems that the individual peasant gardens were quickly producing a large surplus that the peasants were selling on the side in the black market. The Russian government had no explanation.

When I was studying economics in school, I remember a concept that was called "the point of diminishing returns." This economic principle fostered the notion that something could only grow so big before it began to diminish in results - before people began to bump into one another or before "big" got to "unmanageable."

90

When we read our economic history books we find the same notion being advanced and re-advanced from Adam Smith to Galbraith.

There was a time in America when we wanted to bust up trusts and monopolies. But today we have redefined monopolies and disassociated them from "bigness." A monopoly for example is a big business that controls the peanut butter industry from the peanut in the field to the consumer in the market place. But by today's definition if a big business has controlling interests in not only peanut butter but jelly and white bread also, it is technically not a monopoly or a trust - and it is a good thing and not a bad thing. It is a good thing because as we have all been conditioned to believe (erroneously) - big is always better and small is inefficient and wasteful.

The health inspector and a tuna fish sandwich

Spending most of my life in the food service industry, I've met a good many Health Inspectors. But Health Inspection around the USA is by no means a uniform thing. In my experience it not only varies from state to state but from neighborhood to neighborhood. And when you get down to enforcement and interpretation of the laws, it varies from inspector to inspector.

I've met Health Inspectors in big restaurants in Miami. I've met Health Inspectors in chicken factories in Arkansas. I've met Health Inspectors in Meat Processing plants in Massachusetts. I've met them in my butcher shop, in my sandwich shop, at my ice cream stand and in my ice cream parlor right here in uptown/downtown Carrabelle. You would think that with all the Health Inspectors we have all over this country, we would have a fairly safe and healthy food supply. But if you have been watching the news lately, you know that we don't. Unfortunately we don't have any Health Inspectors in Mexico or Honduras - or China and India for that matter. Ah yes, another of the "benefits" of the "Global Economy."

But today I am not thinking globally but locally. I'm thinking of a rather nice, conscientious fellow that once came to inspect my shop over in Carrabelle. This gentleman was all business. He checked everything. He had gauges and thermometers - he inspected inside the building and outside the building. In his previous career he must have be a bacteriologist or a scientist of some sort. He certainly had attention for the details.

But I am happy and proud to report that my little shop impressed him. Twice he found no violations at all in my shop. He told me that didn't happen often. He advised me to buy a frame and pin his squeaky clean reports on the wall in the dining area where my customers could see them. And I did.

When he returned on his next visit and saw that I had followed his instructions, he was thrilled.

But every month he had something new. There was no way to get ahead of this game. These Inspectors were thinking up new plays every day. On this particular occasion that I have in my mind, my man was into salads - like chicken salad or tuna salad. If you had a bowl of chicken salad in your refrigerator, he wanted to know how long it had been there. Any of these type salads would have to be labeled with a date indicating the day they had been prepared.

My wife and I had already conquered this problem. Since we were a little store in a small community, we had to prepare things in very small batches. In fact, my goal was to have a large menu with everything prepared to order - quickly. This was not easy to do. I had worked in a kitchen in the navy preparing food for an "army," as they say. And in Miami and Fort Lauderdale the restaurants I managed had daily waiting lines. My problems prior to Carrabelle had always been not having enough and running out. In Carrabelle I had the opposite problem. I had to devise a large menu to encourage daily business from the same customers and control the waste. I couldn't make a gallon of tuna salad and then end up throwing half of it away.

When it came to the tuna salad, for example, I bought individual cans of white meat albacore tuna - just enough for one sandwich and I mixed the sandwich up with the other ingredients when I got an order.

Well, it seems, the health department was into tuna salad this month. My bacteriologist/inspector had studied my menu and saw that I had a tuna salad sandwich listed, but while searching my prep wagon and refrigerators he found no prepared tuna salad.

"Where do you keep your tuna salad?" he demanded after looking everywhere possible.

"I don't prepare any tuna salad," I told him.

He rushed over to a table and grabbed up a menu. He opened the menu and pointed to my fresh and delicious tuna salad advertisement on the menu.

He finally had me. I could see the gleam in his eye. I must be hiding the tuna salad out in the trunk of my car or some other unhealthy, suspicious place.

"Yes, I have a tuna salad sandwich on the menu but I make it to order."

"How do you do that?"

I took him to my food preparation cart. I lifted a small can of Albacore tuna from the shelf. I showed him a mixing bowl. I pointed to all the various other ingredients that were already in my cart to be used for tossed salads and other sandwiches.

He was totally beside himself. "Wow, that's the best idea I have ever seen," he exclaimed. Obviously he was not an ex-restaurant owner. He probably never worked in a commercial kitchen in his life. When he left my shop that day he promised to bring his wife with him on his day off and get two tuna salad sandwiches.

I couldn't help thinking how strange this all was. Here we were in an age of the local, restaurant chef where the trend was towards home-made everything; where the goal of the small restaurant owner was to give his customers the experience of their life with his own personal secret recipes - homemade sauce, homemade bread and rolls, fresh local ingredients, home grown herbs and spices. And here was the man from the Health Department totally ga-ga over a tuna fish sandwich prepared directly from the can.

Do you think we need some co-ordination here or what?

Settling down in Eastpoint

We lived in a local Eastpoint campground for about 3 or 4 years before we decided to settle down here. To be truthful I think it was my wife who longed for roots more than I did. They accuse women of being "nesters." My wife is definitely a nester - but that is one of her qualities that attracted me to her. She was able to turn every place that we ever lived into a "home." It didn't matter if it was a tiny efficiency apartment in Miami or the back half of a Chevy van.

When she suggested that we start looking around to buy something, I went along for the ride. We owned 40 acres in Arkansas that was just sitting there doing nothing. So why couldn't we own an acre or two here in Eastpoint, Florida - even if we never used it?

Surprisingly, there wasn't much for sale here in Franklin County in those days. Rumor had it that all the "locals" who were land owners were saving their land for the day when the prophesied boom arrived. There were very few realty offices and even fewer "for sale" signs.

We got the name of a couple of prosperous locals and went knocking on doors. I remember one place in particular. It was a nice home, but really nothing compared to the mansions we had all around us in Miami. We were told that this family was the wealthiest in Eastpoint and that they had carpets that were 2 inches thick on their floors. This was meant to be very impressive. Since nearly everybody in Eastpoint oystered for a living we felt no dishonor in approaching the front door of this Eastpoint "mansion" with the 2 inch thick carpets in our white boots and working garb.

We knocked on the front door, a lady peeked out at us through a side window - she didn't appear to be all that excited about our presence. She opened the door a crack. While she looked us up and down, we asked if she had any lots for sale. She looked at us as if we were making a joke. She said no and immediately closed the door.

It seemed that oyster people were not considered good risks back in those days. We actually had enough cash to buy an acre lot just about anywhere in Eastpoint. We didn't want to spend all of it, though.

We got the name of a local businessman who had the reputation of being willing to sell property to oystermen - and on time. His name was Ben Watkins and he had an office in the old Gibson Hotel building. The Gibson had been condemned and was about to be torn down when Mr. Watkins rescued it.

We went over to his office and he actually took us out to look at some of the acre lots he had out on the Wilderness Road - oyster boots and all. The lots were very reasonable. In fact we could have bought two one acre lots or even one 5 acre lot.

We then heard about a man who owned a campground out on the east edge of Eastpoint. He had cleared some land behind his campground and he was also willing to sell to oystermen on time. He had a son-in-law who oystered for a living.

He had three lots available on a dirt road out behind his campground. The road was called the old Escape Rd. We liked the less populated neighborhood. We picked out a lot and made a down payment.

For awhile we just made payments and went out and picnicked on our new lot. It took us about a year to get a septic and a light pole. Then finally we moved from the campground to our lot. We pulled our travel trailer out there and camped. Then a hurricane came and shut the bay down for a whole year. We somehow found part-time work, continued to make our payments and got by with the help of our savings. It was another two or three years before our new mobile home came rolling down our dirt road to be set up on our lot.

Our trailer home was the no frills model - no furniture, no nothing. Our living room was filled with our old lawn furniture. It took another three years before we had our new home and property paid off - we even had a few pieces of conventional furniture by that time.

We have a scrap book with pictures of our mobile home coming down our dirt road to be set up. We have pictures of every new porch or addition that we ever made to our home.

Now we have lived in this little mobile home for 20 to 25 years - rent free. This place doesn't owe us a nickel. Nevertheless, I have been told over the last ten years that my "property" is worth from $100,000 to $200,000. My mobile home is worth nothing but the ground under it is supposedly worth all this money.

I must say, this is all very, very strange.

Oystermen go on STRIKE!

Not too many people probably remember this incident but there was an actual labor strike right here in Franklin County. Someone said that it was the largest labor strike ever in Franklin County. Oystermen in Carrabelle, Eastpoint and Apalachicola picketed every dealer in Franklin County, 24 hours a day for a number of days. I remember the strike lasting a couple or three weeks but my wife says that it was a matter of days. To be honest I don't recall how long it actually lasted.

In 1985 there were two hurricanes: Elena and Kate. The bay was closed to oystering for an entire year. The strike took place as a result of the low prices being offered by the dealers when the bay re-opened. Oystermen demanded at least $10 per bag minimum. The dealers couldn't see it that way, even though they had been paying $15 or $20 per bag for "out of state" oysters all year. The strike took place around the end of 1986 or the beginning of 1987.

Strangely enough labor strikes here in America are not often remembered favorably by the towns, cities, or businesses that were struck. America's historians give labor strikes and protest a very short and terse recording.

I became personally interested in labor strikes several years ago. I found a book at a yard sale that mentioned my hometown of Lawrence, Massachusetts. It credited my hometown with being the scene of one of the biggest and most influential labor strikes in American history. I wondered why I had never heard about it. I was raised in Lawrence and spent 27 years of my life there. How was it that I had never heard of the famous, most documented strike in all of American history? It seemed very strange.

I decided to research the Bread and Roses strike and other important labor strikes throughout American History. I have now accumulated a few hundred pages and I will be publishing a book on this subject.

I thought initially that I would write a book on every important labor strike in American history. In my naiveté I thought that there may have been 50 or so major labor strikes from the colonial period up until today. There were thousands - tens of thousands! Workers were machine-gunned, brutalized, harassed and murdered right here in America - as they are today in third world countries around the world where the battle for respect and fair wages continues.

What I hadn't realized was the fact that there has been a war going on here in the brickyards and parking lots of America ever since this country began. And what is even more amazing nobody seemed to know about it. It certainly isn't being taught in our public schools or universities. As far as I know only Cornell University offers a degree program in the study of American Labor in the United States.

Contrary to common knowledge if it were not for the protests on the part of working people throughout American history what most of us have and enjoy today and consider a part of the greatness of America and its dream would not be.

For example the eight hour work day, the forty hour work week, the paid vacation, any kind of medical insurance or retirement plan, public school education, social security, workmen's compensation, jobs for women and blacks, child labor restrictions, sanitary and healthy work places, decent non-toxic living areas, freedom of speech and the right to assemble, collective bargaining, the right to protest, freedom of the press, decent pays and benefits for soldiers, policemen and firemen and the list could continue. It would not be a stretch to credit the GI Bill and the establishment of the middle class to the efforts of blue collar soldiers who returned from World War II and continued the fight for fair pay and respect right here at home.

All the basic rights that we cherish were pounded into laws here in the streets, alleys and industrial parking lots of America. It was slave uprisings, runaway indentured servants, suffragettes, Planned Parenthood organizers and birth control advocates. It was labor organizations - socialist, communist and capitalist that changed the American family and the life conditions for all Americans.

So, I was just thinking about that strike in Franklin County. I wonder if anybody kept a record of what actually happened. I wonder if anybody today cares that there was a time when a few thousand seafood workers right here in Franklin County were parading up and down the streets fighting for fair wages and respected treatment?

I remember telling several of the dealers at that time that this was the time for them to join in with their workers so that they could present a united front against all the problems that were coming down the road from the State and Federal government. They didn't.

All of those dealers are now out of business. Some of them sold out or bailed out; others went bankrupt or just gave it up. I often wonder if they would still be in business here in Franklin County if they had nurtured those two or three thousand striking seafood workers. Would two or three thousand contented workers fighting for the dealers' rights to stay in business have made a difference? Instead they won the strike against their workers and were able to cut oystermen's wages (bag prices) but they lost the war - and their livelihoods.

Yes, Labor in America has an interesting history. You should read about it - if you can find a book on the subject. I have been hunting for years now. I have salvaged a large collection but you won't find any of them at your local bookstore. The whole story of the American labor movement seems to be a big secret.

Carol and her cast net

Being an Eastpointer, of course, requires knowledge of both cooking and smoking mullet but it doesn't end there. You have got to know how to catch it also.

A traditional, non-commercial method for catching mullet is via a cast net. Cast netting for mullet is an old Eastpointer and Franklin County tradition. My wife Carol was not satisfied learning to catch mullet by throwing a cast net. She wanted to learn to make her own cast net too. And she did.

I really don't remember how long it took her to hand tie this net but it was a long time - a year anyway. She would sit in our camper, or outside by the campfire with her weaving tools and knot by knot tie this throw net. I was not convinced that she would ever really finish it - but she did.

And on this one auspicious Sunday afternoon we went over to Battery Park in Apalach and meandered out onto the pier to give Carol's new cast net a try. My old buddy Ronald the Redneck just happened to be out there with a pretty good Sunday afternoon crowd. I told him all about Carol hand crafting her net. He took a look at it and was mighty impressed.

Carol had been practicing throwing the net. She had finally mastered the technique. She could toss it and make it spread out pretty well on the front lawn. She was quite proud of herself.

So she got herself into the proper position. She had a portion of the net up over her shoulder and the weight line between her teeth and she gave it the old sashay and tossed that thing right out there.

It spread perfectly. It looked beautiful as it floated through the air and then settled on the surface of the water and started sinking rapidly. She had done it perfectly - except for one tiny detail. She forgot to loop the retrieving pull rope around her wrist. So, in effect, she had just thrown her net away. When I saw the rope handle out there floating, I looked at my wife.

Her face was twisted in distress. "Richard! You've got to get it honey?" she pleaded.

How the heck was I supposed to get that darn thing? I had no idea but within a few seconds I was leaping off the pier and into the drink. I remember seeing a tiny piece of the handle of the green colored pull rope momentarily on the surface. I tried to gage my leap off the pier with one arm stretched out to grasp the rope where it had last been.

You won't believe this but no sooner did I hit the water than I felt that tiny rope hit the palm of my hand. I had the darn thing. It was a miracle.

When I came back up to the surface I held the rope up in the air where everybody could see. We had a crowd there now and I got a big cheer.

But the water level was about 10 foot below the level of the pier. I swam over to a wooden piling and tried shimming myself up the pole. I got up the piling far enough that I could hand the rope up to my wife who was lying on her belly and reaching down over the edge of the pier. She was just able to get it and pull her net up. But Dick was still down there clinging to a piling.

I kept trying to shimmy my butt up that pole. I remember shimming up poles when I was a kid but that was when I weighed 42 pounds and not 242 pounds. I was going nowhere fast and it was a long swim down the channel to solid ground.

Ronald the Redneck then appeared over the edge. He bent over at the waist and stretched his hand down to me and said;

"Grab ahold and I'll pull you out."

At first I thought I would do as he said but then it occurred to me that I weighed over 200 pounds, if I grabbed onto his hand with him bent over as he was, why I'd just pull him into the channel on top of me. There was no way that he could reach down from the position that he was standing and pull 200 pounds up onto the pier with one arm. I mean come on!

"Ronald," I said. "I know that you are a big old, strong, country boy but you can't pull me up there. I weigh as much as you do."

"Do you want out of there or don't you?" he said.

"I want out."

"Well then get ahold, like I told you."

I thought Ronald was nuts but I reached up and grabbed onto his hand.

I no sooner got hold of his hand than I was skidding and bouncing up on that pier. I got a sliver in my nose from sliding along so fast. I couldn't believe it.

I rolled over on the pier and I looked up at Ronald who was standing there with a big grin on his face.

"Ronald, if I ever doubt your word again, you just bring me back down to this pier and throw me back in.

"I'll do that," said Ronald. And I know that he will and I also know that he can.

Valedictorian

In the Franklin Chronicle there was a story on the front page a year or two ago. It was about a little girl who just graduated from one of our tiny little High Schools.

Her picture was on the front page along with that of her proud mother. It was a neat little story. This little girl had graduated first in her class. She was the Valedictorian.

She had a grade point average that was ludicrous. I mean on a possible 4.0 she had 4.5 or something. How the heck can that be?

Well she not only completed and excelled at the regular high school stuff but she took preparatory college courses in her "free" time.

It was noted in the little article that she had received a couple of "scholarships." She got a $1000 dollars and $500 from some local charities and $25 from the Mayor or something.

I didn't think much about the story until the next morning when my wife and I decided to go down to the local restaurant for some biscuits and gravy.

The little girl that waited on us looked a lot like the cute little valedictorian whose picture was in the paper. My wife asked her if it was she. It was.

Now that didn't upset me either. Why shouldn't the local valedictorian be working and delivering grits and gravy to the likes of me and the wife? It is good for kids to work and have jobs.

As we chatted affably with the young lady my wife whispered; "You would think that the local Valedictorian would have a scholarship to FSU or someplace?"

It seems that she was going to be attending the local Community College. She was studying nursing. Nursing? Does America need nurses? Dahh ... I guess!

This brought me to my own family and my personal career.

My older sister was Salutatorian from her High School. My sister, who was also a working high school student, got no

104

collage scholarships. Back in those ancient times girls really weren't expected to go to collage anyway. As a single mom, she has worked not one, not two but three different jobs in order to survive.

My older brother was Valedictorian of his graduating class. He, like this little girl, had an impossible grade point average because he passed exams for classes he never even enrolled in. He had the highest grade point average in the history of his high school. He got no offer from colleges either. He worked his way through a couple of years of college on a special "work" program at Northeastern University.

I didn't do all that well in high school but I did get to a Community College and at the end of my first year I was first in my class. I went to the financial aid department and spoke to Dean So and So. When I told him that I had spent my entire life savings on my first year at college, he told me to go to the local bank and get a loan. I was also the child of a struggling single mom - my dad had died when I was just turning into a teenager. I took this comment by the Dean of "Who gives a Flip" as a total lack of interest on his part so I dropped out and got a job driving a truck.

When I had saved enough money I went back to that same Community College. It was a two year school and when I finished, I was once again first in the class. Via this great achievement I received no offers to other universities.

I applied for a college loan as I had been advised previously. I needed at least $3000. On the first week of admissions to the local college, I was called to the student loan department. I was informed that though I was not granted the $3000 that I had applied for - I was granted $300.

I told the nice lady to give the $300 to an applicant whom they felt more deserving and I dropped out of college and got my truck driving job back.

As you can probably understand, I have always been rather skeptical about this Nation's supposed commitment to "Higher Education."

My wife says that my attitude is just sour grapes and my story is ancient history. She says that anyone who wants to go to college in the U.S. today can do so if they want to. I say BULL!

But don't get me wrong, this little girl downtown wasn't griping. She was as happy as a lark. She was all smiles and as proud of herself as could be. But I know how I felt way back when. I had given it my best and no one gave a flying flip.

So what do I expect? Do I think that this little girl from Carrabelle or Apalachicola should be going to Harvard or Yale because she was first in her graduating class of fifty?

No, I guess not. But doesn't she deserve something? You know from the greatest nation in the whole world - the nation that "believes" in its children and thinks that education is the salvation and cure for all of mankind and blaa, blaa, blaaa?

I left the kid a two dollar tip ... my wife made me put down another buck. Three buck TIP for two orders of biscuits and gravy! And so it goes.

Privatization of the Bay

A number of years ago a state program came to our area. The big push at that time was the privatization of anything and everything. Apalachicola Bay was to be divided up into one acre leases and rented to qualified applicants for the purpose of "farming" their own oysters.

The program had numerous problems and large local opposition. Many oystermen along with fishermen, crabbers and shrimpers were very much opposed to any leasing or privatization of the public resources. All the other users of the bay, even the sport fishermen, found the idea problematic.

But I am not interested in rehashing all the arguments that resulted from that program. I want to talk about an idea for developing the bay that never seemed to get off the ground or even get notice.

I had been communicating with a number of universities and research centers with regards to this notion of farming oysters. I had contacted a professor of Marine Biology at FSU among others. His name was Dr. Livingston and he had done considerable research in Apalachicola Bay. While talking to him on the phone he informed me of a book that he had written describing a plan that he devised for the future of Apalachicola Bay and the National Estuary.

He wanted the National Estuary to grow into a marine biology center and eventually establish a nursery and a hatchery. Local high school students would take courses there and get hands-on experience. Marine biology students from FSU would also train and learn at the facility in Apalach. There would eventually be trained managers to run the hatcheries. Oyster harvesting could be improved with bed building and seed planting if it proved viable. Fish hatchling like mullet, spotted sea trout, flounder etc. could be planted. White shrimp, brown shrimp and even blue crabs could be grown and seeded in the bay.

The program could be supported in many ways. As in Michigan and Oregon special stamps could be issued and sold to sport and commercial fisherman alike. The local government, the state, the sport fishing community, tourist fishing, and the commercial fishing industry could all contribute to a healthy and productive bay. Profits could be enhanced and good jobs developed locally.

I thought this was the greatest idea I had heard. Everyone would benefit. All cost would be shared. Profits would be taxed as always but there would be more and more profits. New, good paying jobs for local children would be developed. The existing industries would not be challenged but complimented. Everyone could learn and everyone would prosper.

I wrote letters to the local newspaper and told everybody about this plan of Dr. Livingston but the idea received no attention. A conversation or dialogue never ensued. I could never understand it. Everybody talked of saving and improving the bay but nobody gave this great idea a second glance.

I recently covered the county commission meetings for a few years and I heard lots and lots of talk about the bay. But never once did I hear this idea of a hatchery and science lab ever mentioned.

Carol is originally from Michigan and we spent a good deal of time up there working, visiting and enjoying their fisheries. They developed a network of hatcheries that are credited with saving Lake Michigan. They hatched eggs and planted Steelhead and Salmon fingerlings. It became a fisherman's paradise. Carol and I caught huge Salmon and Steelhead trout on the piers and channel walls and up some tributaries and at the base of different dams. It was quite a thrill to battle with a ten to fifteen pound Coho Salmon or a Rainbow Steelhead trout of equal size.

My guess is that this column will also go unnoticed. The bay has too many problems. If the flow coming down the river isn't improved who knows what will be the result. And once again we are in a period of fiscal restraint. I think that we all have to learn that there is a difference between "investment" spending and other types of government spending. When we invest in something it will one day bring a return to the country in good jobs and increased revenue. This type spending is hardly comparable to pork-barrel spending or building bridges to nowhere. But if there is no investment, private or public, there will be no growth and no improvement. When the private business community stops investing, unfortunately the government must take up the slack or it is back to 1929 and the 1930's.

Our bay is still pretty much of a mystery. No one knows how productive it could be or what capacity it has for all the different species. It would be interesting to find out rather than to stand by and watch it die.

.01 Cent sales tax

The new publisher of the Chronicle, surprisingly enough, has asked me to offer, occasionally, some of my personal opinions on local issues in my new column. Actually this may be the first time in my life that anyone has actually asked for my opinion.

The previous owner Mr. Tom Hoffer encouraged me to work for him because he also said that he would like to print some of my ideas and opinions. But whenever I submitted those opinions he had a problem. He rejected on the average 50% of my submitted opinions and ideas. But to his credit he did relent 50% of the time.

In my past life I usually volunteered my opinions even to strangers, unsolicited. But after a number of years of volunteering I discovered that my friendships were getting fewer and fewer and barrooms became a big problem for me. Like the old joke; "I thought he said stand up and he was actually saying shut up." - and thus I decided to become a writer.

In this way I could vent all of my opinions and ideas and unless some fool decides to publish them, I have no problem. My backup strategy has been the George Washington technique - say as little as possible thus leaving your ignorance to speculation.

My new boss expressed his interest on what I might have to say on the proposed .01 cent sales tax that is being considered by referendum this coming November 6th.

Well, the first question I ask myself is whether or not this is a good thing or a bad thing.

It is clearly a good thing in its overall intent. A local hospital benefits everybody. It, of course, helps the local community; it serves the visiting community; it caters to rich and poor alike; it adds to potential positive growth and development; it helps to keep the good medical people in all the peripheral offices and clinics; it benefits the Realtors and the developers; just like a good school system, it increases everyone's property values, it makes the community more desirable and acceptable to potential new residents and workers, it provides good local jobs - skilled, semi-skilled and unskilled, it is futuristic, it's positive and it's needed and will become even more necessary as the community grows. And last but not least, it is money that will be spent in the United States of America, in this very community, for the benefit of AMERICANS.

Many folks say, Well let's look at the numbers. What's the bottom line? Is this thing going to make a profit or a loss?

Well, the bottom line for doing "good" has always been extremely negative. Trying to do good and make things better has always been a big gamble.

But my bottom line evaluation goes like this; What am I being asked to risk or gamble for the possibility of this good thing?

The answer is ... One penny.

This isn't exactly like risking the family farm. In fact this isn't even in the category of buying a lottery ticket. This "risk" is just about nothing. And everybody is going to share in this cost - residents and non-residents, rich and poor alike.

My next consideration is whether or not the people who are asking for this tax and sacrifice on my part are decent, honest and truly concerned with doing good and improving things in this community or do they have some suspicious underhanded intentions.

I had been assigned to cover the County Commission meetings for a number of years. And this may be putting myself out on a limb but as I have listened to these representatives from the Hospital, whether they have been the administrators and directors, doctors, nurses, EMT workers, laborers and employees, Hospital Board Members, even the interim temporary management team, I have always come to the same conclusion. I don't know if these people have been right or wrong but they are certainly sincere and appear to be honest, straight forward and business like. On the local level, many of these people may in fact be some of the best people that this County has to offer. They are concerned, caring, and always talking about the benefit to others and the community. It don't get no better than that!

And the last thing; what they can spend this money on is outlined in the proposition. By law the money can not be spent for anything not stated in that proposition.

If I had been asked to write that proposition, I would have made it more vague and non-specific to give the hospital and the community more space to move and do different things. From my point of view the proposition is even tighter and more restrictive than I would have liked if I were managing such a project. So I have no beef in that regard.

In conclusion, one penny on a sales tax isn't going to bust my family budget. A local hospital is a good thing that benefits not only the local community - rich and poor - but the visitors and new potential citizens as well.

I don't see what this community has to lose. This is a no brainer for me.

Florida secedes - again!

Well, here we are! The most important primary election in my lifetime - maybe in all of American history. There is a WAR to consider and universal health care. Believe it or not Universal Health Care for all American citizens has been a political issue since as far back as the Wilson administration. For the first time in American history we have a possible woman presidential candidate and a possible black presidential candidate. Of course we have all the usual and ordinary types too. We have one movie star, one semi-bald guy who lisps and spits when he speaks, a couple of guys who formally had their picture on a bottle of hair tonic or snake oil, one guy who looks like Gomer Pyle, one guy who looks like he could have been one of the Three Stooges, one guy who has been through the war, the "Mill" and to hell and back, and a host of other interesting prospects.

But it seems that Florida has decided to secede from the Union once again. This time not with the rest of the South but with the state of Michigan of all places. Needless to say I'm confused.

It seems that our Florida legislature took a "bipartisan" vote and moved up our primary election date. Consequently Democrats have been thrown out of the National Democratic Party and Florida Republicans are half out - or something like that.

I have tried to read up on this to find out exactly what happened but that is not really what I want to know. What I really want to know is who actually did this to me and how do I get rid of them - forever. Is it the Democratic Party, the Republican Party, Governor Crist or the entire Florida legislature?

What the heck happened here?

Our state politicians voted to move up our primary elections but both of their political parties told them that they couldn't do it. So naturally they did it anyway. And now all of us who belong to either party are out or semi-out. We have all somehow become independents. We can vote in the national election but we will not get to pick our candidates in any primary. We can go down and pick someone if we want to, but it isn't going to matter because, as usual, nobody is counting Florida votes – at least not all of them. So what's new? Nobody is campaigning here in Florida except the guy who spits along with a thirty second TV sound bite here and there by a few other hopeful losers. No one is calling me on the phone or asking my opinion, taking out an ad in our newspapers or spending any big political bucks here in our state. I am a nobody. I don't count. I'm invisible. I feel like candidates Kucinich and Ron Paul.

My wife says that this must be against the Constitution. I have consulted my copy of the Constitution but I can't find anything in there about primary elections or political parties. There is some stuff about electing presidents and senators and congressional representatives but none of it has any relevance to today's system. In fact, the Constitution seems to be about how they do it in some other country. I'm not going to get into it, but if you don't believe me get a copy of the Constitution and read it for yourself. Who wrote that thing anyway? It seems like it is about time for the revised edition to come out. Believe it or not it says "revised edition" on the copy I've got. When the heck was it revised 1777? I don't really want them to change anything but how about a couple of footnotes explaining what the heck happened and why what it says ain't what we got; inquiring minds what to know.

My wife told me that she belongs to a political party. I asked her when she attended the last meeting and how much did it cost her to join. She said that you don't have to go to meetings to belong to a particular political party and it doesn't cost anything. She said that you just agree to be a member and you are automatically included in that party. It is kind of like a religion but they don't have any churches, she said.

So I guess that is how it goes. Like religion if you have any complaints you pray to God and if He sees fit, he changes it. Otherwise you end up you know where – and without a paddle.

Pier fishing

We first learned about pier fishing on our adventure Hobo-ing America. When we were bumming around America a convenient seaside pier offered several advantages. The first was, of course, fish, crabs and whatever other type of seafood drifted around under the pier. The next big advantage was free camping. Most piers encouraged all night fishing - or at least didn't discourage it. If the parking was limited at the pier there was usually a tavern or cafe nearby with a friendly owner who welcomed customers and strangers. We camped for a week at a bar and sandwich shop across the street for a beautiful pier in Oceanside California. We caught fish, stone crabs, and we ate delicious yellowfin tuna that we bought from a guy who had a mobile stand and smoked it right there on the pier.

When we retired from oystering, we retired from boating. A nice fellow invited us out on his deepwater fishing boat a few years after we sold Hobo's Ice Cream Parlor. As Carol and I sat on a bench seat with our butt bone being pounded into our sculls, we looked at each other with the same thought in mind. Why are we doing this? We caught a few fish that day but that was the last time we went boating.

We haven't been out on a boat in over 10 years now - but we still fish regularly. We love the Eastpoint fishing pier. Every year we fill our freezer with spotted trout, silver or sugar trout, croakers, flounder, whiting and maybe a few nice redfish. Last season we even caught several messes of Spanish mackerel.

We buy some frozen or fresh shrimp at the local bait and tackle shop in Eastpoint – Fisherman's Choice. We get our rigs and weights there also. I like the two hook leader with the weight at the bottom. Carol uses the one hook rig. It is the same kind of a rig that you would use for fishing in the surf. We buy #4 long shank hooks and a one ounce weight. We bring a five gallon bucket that we drop off the edge and fill with bay water to wash our hands, a net on a long rope that we designed ourselves for bringing up those big ones, a cooler with ice cold

115

drinks and beer that doubles as a fresh fish carrier, two or three fishing poles, a tackle box, and at least one collapsible cloth chair.

And there we sit or stand - cold drinks, snack food, plenty of nice people to talk to, no waves, no expensive gasoline, no boat to wash, no two hour ride out to the "secret" fishing spot, no motor problems, no trailer, no coast guard, no conservation man, no tow boats, no boat insurance, no licenses, no jammed props, no seasickness, no problems.

We consider ourselves "professional" pier fishing people - but there are people out there who are much more sophisticated than us.

We cart all our paraphernalia out onto the pier with an old handcart or warehouse dolly. Some folk have two and three hundred dollar wagons complete with pole holders and fish cleaning boards. We saw two pier professionals last weekend who both had hydraulic carriers on the back of their SUVs. When they were done fishing they simply wheeled their wagons onto their hydraulic carriers - cooler, tackle box, poles and all, elevated their lift and headed back to Georgia, Alabama, Marianna, Panama City or wherever. One lady even had an electronic beeper on her reel that beeped and flashed when she was getting a bite.

Pier fishing supplies us with all we need - a little exercise walking out, usually a cool ocean breeze, a pleasant view of our beautiful bay and estuary, a spectacular sunset, the fun of catching fish, the joy of eating a batch of sautéed, baked or fried fish fillets, limited expense, nice people who enjoy similar excitement, comfort and a firm place to stand - no Dramamine necessary.

I have to laugh sometimes when I see boats pull up right next to the pier. They have the whole bay but where do they come? Right to the pier. The boats are rocking this way and that. When they hook a fish everyone falls all over one another. They are all wearing these three hundred dollar life preservers that are so bulky they can barely manage their poles. Carol and I just smile. What a pleasure it is to be a professional, BOAT-LESS pier fisherman. We've got it made.

116

Franklin County Stories and More

It's Christmas, cheer up!

There are only two kinds of people in the world - those that love Christmas and those that hate Christmas. I have always been a born and bred, true blue, Christmas hater. And I have very good, rational justification for my adherence to such an attitude. But as fate will have it and just to break my chops and bust my bubble, the all-knowing messengers from the above; the designers of the expanding universe; that impossible infinite brain who controls all the planets - sent me a bride whose birthday just happens to fall on ... December 25th.

What do you think of that? You've heard of the odd couple? How about a situation comedy with Ebenezer Scrooge and Santa Claus living in the same apartment?

It happens every year at about this time. My mind starts to search the dark and dingy corners of my bleak, unhappy childhood for all those tales of misery and neglect that linger like scar tissue on my inner personality and my wife starts bouncing around like a little elf, putting up Christmas lights, doing red and green needlepoint things, and playing Dean Martin's "I'll be home for Christmas" around September. That's when I dig out my Edgar Allen Poe, and start making my annual inquires to the suicide hot line number to see if they are taking on any extra help.

I've always figured that I have the perfect attitude to talk to potential suicide candidates. First, I would listen to their terribly depressing story, and then, I'd say; "Well, sounds to me that you have a perfectly good reason for committing suicide BUT ... let me ask you this. If God could do all of this to you, what makes you think that He is going to lighten up if you commit suicide? You must realize that you are a person who is on God's pooh-pooh list - if you know what I mean. Did you ever figure that it ain't gonna get no better than this, and that maybe being a hopeless alcoholic is going to be the high point of your eternity? He put you here and did this to you — do you really want to find out what He has planned next? THINK ABOUT THAT!

119

To tell you the truth, for the first five years or so of our marriage, just looking at my wife's bubbling smile and rosy cheeks at this time of the year, gave me chronic morning sickness. In fact, this year, I've sent for my own home pregnancy test kit. Boy, that's all that I need.

But enough of this fun and games, I've sat down here today to make all of you cry - after all, this is Christmas. But first, I have to get you all in the mood.

Tell me, do you have any retarded children? Anybody in your immediate family have an incurable disease? Did you ever back up out of the drive, over one of your own children? Come on, THINK! You couldn't have lived through all of these Christmases without being miserable at least once in your life. Didn't you ever say, "So what if our little Nancy got bit by a strange dog. How does anybody really know if that was actual saliva foaming around its mouth? And besides, this tetanus shot business is just another plot by Doctors to make themselves a bunch of extra bucks."

So, are you getting into a crying mood yet? No? Then let's think - cancers? terminal brain tumor? unemployment? bankruptcy? stock market crash? hunger? pestilence? poverty? starvation? nuclear fallout? war? global warming? experimental research on the Easter Bunny? That's not a lump, honey; it is just a little fat - too many kielbasa sandwiches, more than likely.

But can you believe this! Do you see what's happening? That's right - my wife is starting to rub off on me. She is beginning to win the battle. I sat down here today to write something depressing. I hoped to make everyone cry, or, at least, get sick to their stomachs and puke. But, instead, all that I can come up with is this light hearted dribble about disease and suicide. I'll tell you; this makes me want to barf! I'm disgusted with myself. I might just as well go write a Christmas list, or hang some silver tinsel.

I'd really like to tell all of you little kids out there that Santa Claus is dead. But, I have recently read that he was a secret witness for the FBI. Seems that he was involved in some political gift-giving bribery scam and the FBI has issued him a new identity. He is presently living under an assumed name in some remote sheep herding village in northern Argentina. Don't expect him this year, boys and girls.

So, you see, nothing is working out for me today. I really don't think that I could depress anyone. Everything that I write about is positive. I think that I will just scrap this whole article, and ask my wife to write something cheery about how it feels to be sixty. I mean, she is the one who was born on December 25th, not me. Oh well, happy birthday, honey.

So, tell me, has anyone in your family ever lived long enough to collect and enjoy their Social Security? Being tied to a chair for abusing your refrigerator privileges, back in the laundry room of some Jamaican nursing home in Miami, doesn't count.

Well, the heck with this – everything that I think of sounds just too Rudolph-like. I guess that I am just going to resign myself to directing my feet to the sunny side of the street and decking the halls with bombs of holly – I mean balls ... that's balls ... I mean boughs of holly.

So okay, have a Merry Christmas.

No more TV!

I've seen the 45 vinyl records come and go, and then the LP. After that I watched the cassette tape flutter and die but I never thought that I'd live to see the TV set pass. But the TV is just about dead - at least in my house. That darn thing is shortly going into the junk pile or out the window. I've had it.

I remember going up to the new appliance store on a cobble stone street in my old neighborhood and helping my mother pick out our new 12 inch Zenith television. It cost 3 or 4 hundred dollars. I don't know where my mother found the money, but we had to have that TV. I had my Red Flyer Wagon we carted it home in. For weeks after I got it home, me and my sister jumped up every morning, ran into the parlor and watched the test pattern. Actually now that I think about it, the test pattern was about as good as many of the shows we have on the tube today.

In recent years they nicknamed it the "boob-tube" and it was certainly appropriate - even though there is no longer a tube anywhere in the darn thing.

One of the biggest shows on today's boob tube is called "Boobs with a View" I think. I can't stand it! A bunch of women screaming and yelling at one another. But, if you change the channel you get a bunch of dopey men doing the same thing. It is beyond my capacity for tolerance. But that is not why the TV is coming to an end in my household. It is the cost of this foolishness.

I remember when I was a kid sitting up on the street corner, we used to talk about how one day they would trick us somehow into paying for this TV crap. We used to say; What are they going to do, put a coin collector on it like they have on the bus. We all laughed and concluded that it was impossible. BUT THEY HAVE DONE IT!

I can hardly believe it!

I think when it started out in this neighborhood it was about ten or twelve dollars a month for Cable TV. The picture was clearer than the old antennae and they were going to give us a bunch of new stations along with all the old stuff.

But gradually this Cable Company has gone the way of the automobile - if you want any "extras" it costs more. You know ... did you want a bumper on that pickup truck? How about headlights?

What? What is this?

So now if I want sports, I pay extra; if I want local news, it's extra, if I want movies, it's extra. We don't even get the Gillette Friday night fights anymore. What happened to boxing?

In any case, when the monthly charge got to 50 bucks, I told my wife, TV is over - find a new hobby. Learn to crotchet or make cute things out of plastic wrappers. I know that some of you people are paying a hundred dollars per month or more for TV. You people should be arrested and isolated somewhere on a farm in North Dakota. But my wife couldn't do without the Boob Tube View. She begged and argued. We compromised. We canceled all the extras and went back to the basic. The basic was once again twelve dollars a month. Okay so what's twelve dollars a month? I pay more than that for cat food. But as time slips by the "basic" keeps creeping up. I guess they think that I'm not going to notice - BUT I DO!

Last month I peeked at the bill and the basic was $27.68. This is ridiculous!

Do you know that Diane Sawyer makes something like 13 million dollars a year? Are you kidding me? And Katie what's-her-name makes more than she does. And Barbara Wawa makes more than all of them in a bunch.

Man, I'll bet I could get ten blonde Vassar graduates who could juggle in the nude and read the news at the same time for half that much money. And the men are just as bad. Bill O'Reilly makes a triple fortune. And all these Million Dollar Babies complain about the baseball players making too much money!

The weather guys are millionaires!

Do you remember when they first hired that big, chubby, white guy who made jokes and kept seeking out people who were older than dirt? The other network couldn't be outdone so they hired a big, chubby, bald headed, BLACK guy who also told jokes. These guys are making millions.

I need million dollar entertainment with my weather? I don't even need a weatherologist or whatever they call one of those guys. A simple "It's going to rain or it will be warm today" is good enough for me. Find some unemployed teenager who doesn't lisp and give him 500 bucks a week. He'll never leave.

So okay you cable Mafiosi, when my bill for "basic" hits 30 bucks the TV is gone! And you TV people can take your new digital high definition and put it wherever you feel is appropriate. You say I will no longer know what is going on in the world today. I got news for you - I don't know now what is going on in the world today even with all your help!

So Diane, you will have to take a two cent a year cut when I throw out my TV. I'm sorry; get a part time job. I hear Wal Mart is looking for cashiers.

Greenspan had my job

My editor has advised me that my Eastpointer column should be concerned with local people and local problems or at least have some tie-in to the local community. Soo...

I once knew an oysterman who looked exactly like Alan Greenspan. And speaking of Alan Greenspan, I have several Eastpointer type observations to offer.

Being a student of economic thought and theory, I have been listening to Alan Greenspan give his lectures on TV for years and I even purchased two or three of his past publications. My analysis of Mr. Greenspan has always been: What in the world is that man talking about?

I would sit in front of the TV and make a call for silence in the room each and every time Mr. Greenspan would appear on the TV giving his economic address to the Congress. I would listen to every word assiduously, determined to get the message from the Prophet.

After he would finish, my wife would ask, Richard what did he say? My usual answer went something like this: Well, he said that the economy is good and bad and that it has a tendency to go up and down; those who can afford to wait should and those who can't shouldn't; he said that we should all be concerned and worried but that we should retain our faith in the fundamentals of economic thought and not panic; he said that some people will probably benefit and that other people probably won't.

"And what has all of that got to do with the price of tea in China?"

Well, actually he did mention the price of tea in China and he said that it may go up but that there were extraneous forces that indicated that the possibility of a downward trend due to tea coming from Nairobi could possibly be an influence giving some concern to Chinese tea exporters but Americans who drink primarily black tea which comes from the lower regions of Botswana really have no need to be overly concerned - but of course Britain is an entirely other story.

125

"So basically he said nothing?"

"Exactly."

Now recently Mr. Greenspan has appeared on TV to tell the nation that for his entire stay at the Federal Reserve he has in effect said nothing. He admitted that over the years he has purposely said nothing because for him to say something would have put the onus of responsibility for the future world economy on his shoulders.

Now, in response to questions about his job at the Federal Reserve he explained that as head of the Federal Reserve he tried his best to do as little as possible since he is an avid believer in the Laissez Faire philosophy.

So basically as head of the Federal Reserve he did and said nothing and now he has just written a book that is selling by the millions explaining why he did nothing and how his doing and saying nothing has benefited the nation and the world.

I have come to the conclusion that this man had my job. Alan Greenspan made big bucks for doing this job where he did and said nothing by his own admission. But he actually earned nothing when compared to what he would have made if he had remained in private enterprise where I imagine he would have had to do and possibly say something. But, of course, he can't tell us what he would have said and done if he had remained in private enterprise because his revelation of such information would change the course of the economic world.

Where do I apply for that position? I can do that.

Every place and position that I have ever held in my life others have accused me or said flat-out that I was doing nothing and that what I had to say about what I was doing amounted to nothing whatsoever.

I certainly have the resume' to fulfill the position as head of the Federal Reserve Bank of America following the Alan Greenspan guidelines. I can do and say nothing with the best of God's creatures - just give me the chance and stand back and watch me not do anything. Actually, just keep reading this column and see if you can point out where anything that I have ever said has ever accomplished more than nothing whatsoever. Clearly the proof is in the pudding.

There is no inflation

I don't want to upset all you retired folks out there but I have found out that the Government has been lying to us about inflation.

I know, I know, you are all shocked. You can't believe I could actually come right out and say the U. S. Government is lying. I am sure some of you think I should be charged with treason and sent to a foreign country to be tortured. I know to actually believe our government would lie is really hard to swallow. There must be some other explanation? Maybe it only appears that they are lying? Maybe I have misinterpreted the facts? Well, I'll let you be the judge.

Inflation is interpreted by the government as CPI. The CPI is the Consumer Price Index. This index was once calculated by comparing the prices of a certain group of goods and services from time to time and then estimating the increase or decrease in their costs. This task was performed by the BLS, the Bureau of labor Statistics. As the cost of everything in this so called basket of goods and services kept rising, the government decided that something had to be done. Something had to be done because this method was costing the government too much money in cost of living adjustments to retirees, retired veteran's pensions, Medicare payments, government employees, bond holders and whatever. So they appointed somebody named Boskin and instructed him to form a commission and study this problem.

If you are retired, receiving a pension, have your life's savings invested in government bonds, working under a government contract, or anything that is adjusted for inflation by somebody and you now find that you can only afford to buy half a tank of LP gas, or you can no longer afford to drive your car more than one block in any direction, or you are wondering if cat food can be consumed by humans, you can thank Michael Boskin and his Commission. He and his commission rearranged the methods for estimating the Consumer Price Index.

Mr. Boskin had some "overlooked" economic concepts that he brought into the CPI evaluation like; substitution, hedonics - quality estimations, geometric weighing, seasonal adjustments, along with the elimination of certain incalculable volatile variables like energy, food and local, state and federal taxes. So, for example, when the CPI was calculated without consideration for food, energy and taxes it was often found that there had been no inflation at all. Wow! Isn't that great?

So you ask; why is it that I don't have enough money to live on any more? Well, obviously you are still heating and cooling your home, eating food and paying your taxes. If you will just stop doing those things you will find that you have just as much money as you always had.

But just in case that wasn't enough to bail out the government, Mr. Boskin thought up a few other safety measures to guarantee that inflation didn't go up.

One of his measures he called "substitution." In other words if the price of beefsteak in our typical basket of goods went up from the last time that Mr. Boskin went shopping, he substituted hamburger; and if hamburger was too high he substituted chicken; and if all the meat was too high; he substituted vegetables; and if vegetables were too high one can imagine that Mr. Boskin would have us consumers check out the ingredients on a bag of Friskies. Then, of course, we don't have to buy the name brand Friskies, we could buy Gritskies and we don't have to buy Ritz Crackers we can buy Fritz or Blitz Crackers.

Next on Mr. Boskin's list of improvements was "hedonics" or quality compensations. Let's say that Mr. Boskin bought a TV for $329 on his previous expedition and then on his following survey the same model TV cost the exact same price. But the new TV had a better picture, was estimated to last 2 years longer, and due to improvements in technology it had a much better sound. Mr. Boskin figured that even though RCA chose not to charge us for these improvements the government had no obligation to be so generous. Mr. Boskin estimated, for example, that these improvements were worth in terms of quality enhancement, $135. He therefore calculated that a new

TV didn't really cost the consumer $329 but only $194. As you can plainly see our CPI actually went down instead of remaining exactly the same.

But hedonics only seems to travel in one direction. If you personally don't benefit from these new technological wonders because you have grown old and your vision and hearing have diminished or even if you didn't need and don't want the new and improved model, you still get billed by Boskin, nonetheless.

I could explain to you Mr. Boskin's "geometric weighing" as opposed to the old antiquated arithmetic method and his seasonal adjustments but I don't really think it is necessary. I think that most of you out there will agree with me when I say that Mr. Boskin and the U.S. government who hired him are not simply spinning the truth but are really telling lies.

Education is the answer?

In my "gallivanting" about town, and even out of town, I have noticed in all of my favorite stores - the Dollar General, Bill's, Piggly Wiggly, the IGA, Wal-Mart, K Mart and numerous others, there is often a solicitation of some kind for "education." They don't want to educate old people like me - who are almost dead anyway and for whom a better education would be superfluous; somewhat like slopping caviar to the hogs, I guess. They want to educate young people so that they will be able to get a "good" job when they grow up.

I wonder if these businesses realize that if their education drive is truly successful, they will go out of business.

Certainly if you study hard, get that good education and go to college, hopefully you will not be working at Bill's, or the Dollar General, or Wal-Mart or K Mart. You will get a "good" job not a "regular" job.

If all our children get a good education who is going to do all the "regular jobs" that comprise 80% of the jobs available in the "real" American economic world ... illegal aliens? It is also interesting to note that this 80% of American jobs is provided by "small businessmen" and not large corporations. Many small businessmen can't even afford Workmen's Compensation never mind health and retirement benefits – this is called "Supply and Demand." Thirty percent of our present labor force is now contract labor, freelance independents, self-employed and working at home – read no insurance and no benefits.

And furthermore, if all of our children are able to get a good education, then, of course, a "good education" will no longer be of any value - because everybody will have one.

If everyone has a good education then everyone will qualify for all the good jobs. In which case, the pay for the good jobs will then drop and the good jobs will not be so good anymore. This is already happening. Competition from educated young people coming from India and Asia are making the world of the American college educated more and more challenging.

130

But, on the positive side, I suppose that if you have a good education you will then be smart enough to understand why you are now unemployed. I suppose that could be looked at as a step in the right direction.

As we all should know, we live in a capitalist/competitive society. In this type society what you really want is a good education for your child and a lesser education for your neighbor's child. In this way, your child becomes the manager of the Bill's or Wal-Mart and your neighbor's child gets to gather up the shopping carts in the parking lot.

George Will and others tell us that the solution to "poverty" is education. George thinks that we can educate people out of poverty (and teenagers out of pregnancy).

Sure you can educate YOUR child out of poverty. Yes, you can educate A PARTICULAR CHILD out of poverty, but after he/she graduates from poverty, the state or institution of poverty still remains. New lesser educated people move into those poverty positions. As long as there remain places where people do not earn a living wage there will be poverty. If you educate every human being in the entire world but continue to pay people wages on which they are unable to sustain themselves - you will simply have well educated people starving to death in ghettos and slums around this country and the world.

So, is education a good thing? Of course it is.

Should you want a good education for your child? Sure you should. Do you want everybody's child to get an education equal to that of your child?

Well, I suppose you don't really have to worry about that because everybody's children are all not capable of getting a good education. Some of our children will only be qualified to gather the shopping carts in the parking lot no matter how much education we attempt to drive into them. I met an American kid the other day who was so slow, I commented to my wife; "That boy is either severely mentally challenged or he is a very tall two year old." And what happens to all these type children in America?

Truly, do you want to live in a country or a world where everything is fair or in one where you and yours have a special advantage? I think we all know the answer to that question.

That special advantage can be inherited wealth or inherited genetic potential and I'm sorry but neither can be considered "fair."

Four vanilla

It seems when this old buddy of mine was a child his dad took him and his siblings for a ride to the ice cream parlor that was on the outskirts of his hometown. This event, of course, got the kids all excited. The father, in order to keep the kids occupied, would ask the children to perform the same task every week. "Now kids, I want you to be thinking of what flavor ice cream cone you are each going to order. We don't want to keep the lady waiting when we get there. She is always very busy."

The kids immediately went into their flavor discussions.

"I'm going to get a strawberry ... no, no I think I'll get a black cherry."

"I'm going to get a frozen pudding."

"Ouu, ouu, I'm going to get orange pineapple or maybe a fudge ripple."

"I think I'll get banana or maybe cherry vanilla."

All the way out to the ice cream stand the kids jabbered and discussed their possible choices enthusiastically. When the car finally stopped at the much anticipated destination, all the kids rushed out of the car and followed daddy up to the window. When pop got to the window, without the slightest hesitation and no consultation whatsoever, he placed his order.

"We'll have four vanillas please."

All the kids frowned and sulked as they licked their vanilla ice cream cones all the way home in silence.

Every time I think of that story I laugh. I'm sure it was a traumatic experience for my friend Eddie and his brothers and sisters, but I can see where the dad was coming from also. If all four children didn't get the same thing they would be arguing and fighting all the way home. The car would be a mess; the kids would all be screaming and crying; the whole trip would end up a disaster.

And this all brings me to our local County Commissioners.

A while back a fellow came to the County Commission meeting and accused the commissioners of "earmarking" the

County Budget. This was rather humorous. Three of our five County Commissioners didn't even know what earmarking was. The County Planner had to explain the principle of earmarking to them. I think our critic was watching too much C-SPAN

Earmarking is what goes on in Washington D. C. and Tallahassee and it is the term used for the technique by which Congressmen and Senators secretly encode their home pet pork-barrel projects into the various legislations. It is really a very complicated process on the Federal level and it takes a budget large enough to hide things. Recently a group of young journalists have been studying the process and it has been no easy effort to unmask all the inveiglement and deceptive practices.

Most pork-barrel spending is money that is spent here at home - minus whatever was not outright stolen along the way. If it is cut from the budget what will happen to the money?

The pork-barrel critics think that by cutting pork and even domestic spending somehow the government will end up with a surplus and all the faithful taxpayers will then get their money back.

Well surpluses don't happen very often. Bill Clinton claimed a surplus in 1998 of $69.2 billion. This was the first supposed surplus in over forty years. But if the $99.2 billion Social Security Surplus gained from the 1983 increase in the Social Security tax is subtracted, Clinton actually had a 30 billion dollar deficit. In 1983 an increase in the Social Security tax was mandated to compensate for the future flood of baby boomers. In 1999 when Clinton claimed a $124.6 billion surplus, it seems that the actual surplus was 1.9 billion after the baby boomer Social Security Surplus of $123.7 billion was subtracted. The most significant surplus in the Clinton years was in 2000 when an on budget surplus of $86.6 billion was actually achieved. Of course Clinton added in the old folk's pension once again and came up with a surplus of over $230 billion.

All this surplus money then led George the Lesser to decide that the federal government had too much money, so he sent the old timer's Social Security money to all of his rich buddies

- sort of a CEO bonus plan. Now, once again they can scream and yell about cutting benefits to the old folks.

We have two political philosophies today. We have the tax and spend Democrats and the borrow and spend Republicans. Actually the borrow and spend Republicans are much worse economically than the tax and spend Democrats ever dreamed of becoming. Ronald Reagan borrowed and spent enough to increase our National Debt to double what all of the previous presidents from George Washington forward had accomplished. Bush the Major doubled the debt that Ronny had amassed and now Bush the Lesser is trying his best to out borrow and spend his dad.

So it looks to me that whether we have a Democrat or a Republican spending will continue. There will be no "four vanilla" type thinking or simple solutions. It will be every flavor under the rainbow and the squabblers will squabble endlessly. It is inevitable; our history assures it. And if the spending is going to continue I would rather have it spent on pork here at home than fat and pure lard abroad.

Water wars?
No exaggeration!

Just recently in our tiny fishing village by the bay, we had a battle over water in Lanark Village. The problem is said to have been solved. We all hope so. It seemed like a personality conflict to most citizens but in the middle of the fight one Lanark Commissioner brought up the notion that this whole thing could actually be a "water grab" by private enterprise.

On the west side of our tiny metropolis we have what also could be considered a "water grab" over our Apalachicola River. I say "our" river but as most of us already know there are two other states who also consider the Apalachicola River their property.

One might think that these water grab problems are a local phenomenon. Well this is far from the case. Water is becoming a big problem all over the world. It is not just the Apalachicola River that is trickling down to a stream but the Colorado, the Nile, and rivers everywhere.

Lake Mead out West may be drained in less than five years some predict. New Mexico has three to five years left and its drinking water will be gone. California has a decade or maybe two.

The privatization of water supplies and sources is getting serious. Coca Cola, Pepsi and Nestle Company are the new OPEC of world water supply. Soda pop companies are being run out of villages and countries in South America and around the world. The World Bank is admitting that its encouraging of the privatization of the water supply of third world countries by international conglomerates was a mistake. Coca Cola is accused of assassinating union leaders at their bottling plants in Columbia. There is a political battle going on between Pepsi and Coke for power to control the Mexican government. There are actually soda pop wars - with guns, bullets, killings, and revolutionaries.

Drinking water around the world is running out. If Global warming is the problem of the century, drinking water is considered by many to be the problem of the decade. Some activists are claiming that privatization of the world's drinking water could not only result in genocide but in the disappearance of the human species entirely. Agribusiness and ethanol are even presenting a problem. Unfortunately it takes water to grow corn and other renewables.

GE has already begun desalinating the ocean. Could the oceans actually be drained? Well think Aral Sea in Russia. The Aral Sea was once the forth largest lake in the world. It stretched 266 miles. The Russians instituted a farm irrigation project. Today the lake level has dropped over 70 feet. It contains ¼ of its original volume. This is considered one of the greatest man made environmental disasters in human recorded history. And it may be impossible to reverse. It is gone. Imagine the Great Lakes in the U.S. gone.

The Chinese are building a water pipe line to the top of the Himalayas. There are fears that in feeding water to China the Chinese may kill the entire river systems of Asia.

This all sounds like something out of a science fiction movie but it is not. This is the real thing. There is a documentary film coming out soon. It is entitled FLOW - for love of water by Irena Salina. A woman by the name of Maude Barlow has written several books on the subject also. Her latest book is Blue Covenant and it follows her previous publication entitled Blue Gold.

A corollary to all of this is the bottled water business. Do you feel healthier drinking bottled water? Do you feel you are benefiting the environment - that you are doing the "right" thing?

Well, supporting the bottled water industry may not only be unhealthy and environmentally unsound but you may also be contributing to the violent take over of the third world's water supply, the extortion and exploitation of the poor and the illegal and immoral corporatization and privatization of the world's water supply, say some experts.

137

The plastic bottles are not biodegradable, which some may consider a minor point. Ninety-five percent of them are not being recycled. They are filling up the landfills. The stoppers are even worse. The water in these bottles may not be safe and it is not being inspected or certified by anybody. With the help of our de-regulation policies of the last thirty years it seems that there is actually one guy in Washington in charge of certifying bottled water - but he is also in charge of several other departments. The consensus of opinion is that there is no one who can verify for you that any bottle of water is safe to drink. It has been admitted by many bottled water suppliers that their water is really filtered tap water. But there are others that come from private sources that no one can certify or verify.

If you are one of those who thinks that privatization is the way to go and that corporate America or Global Corp. does it better, you may want to take a look at the bottled water business. You may be revising your political philosophy for the future.

Medicare – free health insurance!

I will be turning 65 years old in a few months. For the first time in my life I will be eligible for some kind of health insurance. I guess I have always been eligible, I just couldn't afford it. But now because I am 65 I am a candidate for Medicare - "free" health care. Wow, isn't that great? I can't believe it.

But for all you Baby Boomers behind me, I will review what I have found out so far.

First of all Medicare comes in several parts. It is kind of like an alphabet puzzle. There's Part A, Part B, Part C, Part D and possibly some other parts that I am not aware of yet. It seems that part A of the Medicare is the "free" part. I haven't really read what Part A actually covers but who cares - it's free.

Part B is going to cost me $100 dollars a month. It is also going to cost my wife $100. That's $100 per month ... each. Okay, so that's $200 per month. But what if I don't have $200 per month? Don't worry they will deduct it from my Social Security check. So now our already meager Social Security income will be reduced by $200 per month.

But the $200 per month doesn't cover all my potential medical bills. It only covers 80%. So I need to buy another policy to cover what the Medicare isn't going to pay. This is called a Medigap policy. Medigap policies are varied alphabetically also and they run from A through L.

"A" is the no-frills not much better than nothing category. B is slightly better than A and C is the slightly better than B. B costs more than A and C is a little too much for anybody. After C it is Disney World and Never Never Land.

Any Medicap policy will cost me between $100 and $300 per month. That is $100 to $300 each. My wife will need her own policy. And that is in addition to the $100 each that we are already paying for Part B. But even if you can afford F or J you still won't be covered for everything. And no matter what you pay this year it can all go up next year. You must also watch out for the way your Medigap policy is rated. It can be community rated, issue rated, or attained age rated. It could cost you big bucks if you don't find out what these ratings mean. And once you start paying your Medigap insurance company don't stop. If you stop for more than 63 days you will have to be "reborn."

But unfortunately a person is still not covered for any drugs that he might need. And drugs involve co-payments and "donut holes." The co-payment means that I still have to pay some of the costs even if I have the insurance. Let's just skip the donut holes for now - it's too complicated. But basically a donut hole means more money that I have to pay even if I have all this insurance.

For me to be insured against drug co-payments and expensive drugs will cost me another $40 to $100 per month. You can't buy donut hole insurance even if you work at Dunkin' Donuts.

So, that's another $40 to $100 each.

So where are we here? I need $200 for me and my wife for Part B. I need $200 to $600 for what part B doesn't cover. I need $100 to $200 for co-pays and phenomenal drugs with no donut holes. We need $500 to $1000 per month in order to be covered by Medicare.

Unfortunately I can not afford this "free" insurance any more than I could afford the "free-enterprise" insurance. In fact I don't see much difference between the free insurance and the pay insurance. I can't afford either of them.

But we do have other options. We can pay the $200 per month for Part B and get a special insurance by some insurance company (probably with a main office in China or India) that has teamed up with the U.S. Government and Medicare. They will take over the management of my Medicare Insurance. This is some form of "privatization" thought up by the Bushomanics, I presume. With this special policy I will be covered for some things and not covered for a bunch of other things that I will have to pay "out-of-pocket." If I have any problems I will have to fight this Hong Kong insurance company rather than call my

Congressman. This ploy lets my Congressman off the hook. And if I get hospitalized for any length of time I owe somebody $3500 minimum. If my wife and I both get sick at the same time we will owe this person or group $7000 each year.

I have another option though. I could skip the "free" Medicare insurance entirely and keep all of my Social Security check. If I get sick I can die - just like they used to do in the good old days; or I can go to the hospital and tell them to send me a bill. If I don't die from the MRSA infection or Septicemia infection that I catch at the hospital (195,000 people die every year from things they picked up while in the hospital or from medical mistakes), I can get a job – if anyone will hire or pay me in my sick and advanced age, or I can send them payments from my Social Security check.

In the meantime, we can take the $200 per month that we didn't send to the Government for Part B and go to Biloxi once a year and see if I can win a jackpot. Maybe if I win a jackpot in Biloxi I will have enough money to buy some "free" Medicare insurance. Of course maybe with the fines and penalties for joining late, I won't be able to afford it then either - even with the jackpot money.

It's an 'upside-down' world

There is a new concept floating around out there in the world of economics. It's called the "upside-down" people.

If you went down to the new car dealership to trade in that old clunker that you bought four years ago and you found out that you still owe more money on that secondhand car than the car's current estimated value - you are one of the upside-down people.

If you have a home that you have been making payments on for the last ten or fifteen years and you are trying to sell it but you have found out that you still owe more on the house than you can sell it for - you are one of the "upside-down" people.

These were the only two upside-down situations that I read about but I find that there are many others that I have noticed myself.

For example, you decide that you want to participate in the American dream and you open up your own little business. You will learn very quickly that you had better have some Workman's Compensation insurance for Billy, Bob, Susan and Arthur, your employees, in case they get injured or hurt on the job; you will also find that you need accident insurance for your customers just in case one of your customers trips over one of your employees, sprains her ankle and damages her expensive Oprah designer high-heels. But if you or your mate - the owners of this business - trip over one of your customers who then falls on top of an employee of yours, more than likely you (or your spouse) will be the only ones who aren't covered because you can't afford the personal owner's coverage. I don't know but, I think that is slightly "upside-down."

Now let's say that you are a patriotic young boy or girl and you want to do your part for your Country in this time of stress - so you join a branch of the armed services. Now I realize that the pay and salaries for servicemen are much better than they have ever been in the history of this country but if you get a job working for a civilian outfit that has now become a part of the "privatization" of the "new war" concept; you can make considerably more money than any soldier - possibly more than many of the officers and maybe even more than some of the generals. And, I have been told, it is all tax free. Now believe me I am not aspiring or applying for either of the above mentioned positions and I hate to sound like Andy Rooney here but doesn't that seem somewhat "upside-down"?

Now here's another one; you decide that you want to become a doctor. A doctor has always been a respected profession in this country. But in the last few decades I have noticed what appears to me to be a new class of "blue-collar" doctors. These people went to college; they studied hard; they put in their internship and whatever but in order to accomplish this dream they are now nine million dollars in debt from college loans. And not only that, they no longer hang out their shingle or open their practice - they work as an employee for some business school manager or economics major who doesn't even know how to take his own blood pressure. This seems rather upside down to me.

I know young people who finally graduated from college at an age where the young people of my generation would have been married for about eleven years and had three kids. They now have a job where they make three times the highest pay that I have ever had in my life. But they still can't meet their expenses and pay off their college loans. Some of their loans have actually increased since they graduated from college because of accumulated interest due to unpaid principal. I have been saying for years that the only hope for a young girl in this situation is to find a doctor to marry. But she better find an old fashioned white collar, professional doctor and not one of these blue collar doctors like the ones mentioned above.

And now we come to the biggest upside-down in American history. We have something like three million active duty soldiers. I would guess that we have close to that number in our "privatized" military service. We have thirty million retired military. We have tens of millions of workers employed in military procurement and military defense industries here and abroad. If we add up all of our citizens involved in Military in one capacity or another, the percentage would be shocking to most Americans.

If the concept of war would somehow disappear from the human horizon tomorrow, we here in the United States would have to continue producing and manufacturing weapons for another decade or two - even if we just throw them away as opposed to "donating" them abroad - because not to do so would result in a massive economic depression. The economic ship of state, along with the Military Industrial Complex, simply can't be stopped or turned around that quickly. That really sounds upside down to me.

Wash your hands

I have been in the restaurant business or working in some type of food service for most of my life. I have been involved in food from the field to the dining room table; I picked it, I packed it, I processed it, I delivered it, I prepared it, I cooked it, I served it, I sold it - you name it, I did it. But here I was at the Florida Food Service Health and Sanitation Training Program. The State of Florida and several other like-minded States had come to the conclusion that a restaurant was not a healthy place to eat - primarily because of people like me and many others who worked in these unhealthy establishments. Not necessarily because we were dirty, unwholesome, slovenly, derelict, illegal, diseased, unhealthy or had been living under a bridge or sleeping in someone's hedges, but because we were lacking in food handling knowledge. I for one considered this to be a definite step in the proper direction.

There was a very nice man conducting the lecture. He looked normal. He spoke ... normal. He seemed like the kind of a person that you might have living right next door. He was dressed nicely. He was wearing a tie and a suit jacket. He spoke well and had lots of funny little stories about the restaurant business and preparing and eating food. But it soon became obvious that he considered a restaurant equivalent to a toxic dumpsite. By the time that this man had finished his lecture I realized that operating "a healthy" restaurant was an impossibility.

Raw Chicken, for example, should really not be touched. If you must touch it, it should be boiled first. If for some insane reason, you touched a piece of raw chicken before you boiled it, unfortunately, you must now be boiled. If you do not boil yourself within a reasonable time after touching a piece of raw chicken, you will probably die. Even worse than that, you may be the cause of some innocent person's death - possibly even a small child or a dog or a cat.

Hamburger? Hamburger is a very scary material. How and why people ever started using hamburger as a food product is a

145

study for historians and anthropologists. Hamburger needs its own building. If you make a hamburger patty and then touch a piece of raw chicken, you could spontaneous combust. The man showed a slide program of people who instantly exploded while standing in front of a twenty thousand dollar stainless steel sink.

Any utensils that are used in processing any raw meat product must be destroyed after using or sent to Nevada to be buried miles under the ground. And the people living in Nevada must never be told that these utensils are buried in their state otherwise it could cause a panic.

Any and all raw meat products are extremely dangerous but cooked meat products aren't much better. Chicken salad, tuna salad, shrimp salad etc. should be eaten simultaneously with their preparation - or sooner. If you must let a shrimp salad or chicken salad sit in a refrigerator before serving - it should be blast frozen first.

Mayonnaise, ketchup, mustard and other condiments are perfectly safe as long as they are kept in hermetically sealed unopened containers or air tight packaging. If for any reason you must open any of these type containers or packages they should be immediately discarded - or buried in Nevada. Once again, please don't tell any of the people in Nevada about any of this stuff.

Heating things in a restaurant is extremely problematic. Anything heated by an open flame or by convection or convention should reach an internal temperature of 642 degrees Fahrenheit or higher and then should be thrown away before serving.

If you must "hold" something that has been heated for any length of time you should wear heavy Teflon gloves or have an assistant do it – preferably an illegal immigrant.

You should have no unhealthy people working in your restaurant - that includes hunchbacks, midgets, and the cross-eyed.

If you would like to know more about the do's and don'ts of the restaurant business, you can get a free 9,253 page booklet from the Department of Agriculture and Consumer services. If you live in Florida ask for Jerry. If you live anywhere else in the United States ask for Bob - if Bob isn't there ask for Evon.

After the instruction course ended, I had to go to the men's room - the instructor had the same problem and was at the bathroom door just ahead of me.

He took a clean handkerchief out of his breast pocket and wrapped it around the bathroom doorknob. Upon entering the facility he went over to the sink turned on the hot water and washed his hands. He closed the lever that operated the water at the sink with his elbow. After stepping up to a urinal and doing his business he returned to the sink once again and repeated the original procedure. He pressed the button on the hand dryer with his elbow, then once again opened the door with his handkerchief and exited the bathroom.

After listening to this man for three hours and watching his men's room procedure, I had one thought that wouldn't go away; how did this man have sex?

Wow, being privy to a visual of that would be a real study in modern day sanitation and human ingenuity. I can only imagine – but I will try not to.

Meatballs make for poor policy

Back in the good old days in Franklin Country, before the Humane Society, our area out on the Escape Road (now C.C. Land Rd.) was the dumping ground for everybody's castaway pets. At least once a month we had new uninvited guest here in our boonie paradise.

It was always a traumatic experience for us. What do we do with a whole box of little kittens that were in the ditch; what do we do with a limping, mange invested dog; what do we do with a cute little brown and white mutt infested with fleas and ticks?

Oftentimes we set ourselves up with a "Free Kittens" box outside the Eastpoint Post Office, and other times we camped out in front of Register's Supermarket. If those options failed - it was out to the dump or the woods.

It wasn't really very much fun.

One day we found our bunch of acceptable, domesticated well-fed cats had another little stray kitten cornered in our toolshed. I refused to take another living creature to the dump but we could not afford to care for another animal and provide it with the full benefits of the Noble civilization. No way could we provide it with all the necessary shots etc. to enroll it as a citizen in the Noble household. So we made a compromise. We would cut a hole in the toolshed door and leave food for it each day. We called the cat in the toolshed, Meatball. We would feed it but not love it. We would avoid petting it or talking to it. We would let it stay but it would have no household privileges. We would provide it food and shelter until it grew big enough to go off on its own.

Meatball seemed to be doing fine. As he got bigger he fought his way out of the toolshed and into the yard. Our accepted cats didn't make this process easy for Meatball, but Meatball learned how to cope.

As it conquered the yard it gradually worked its way over to the main house. We wouldn't let it in. And even in the springtime when we often had the doors open, it would sit on the stoop and peer into the kitchen longingly. He was rather cute in a sad way. Every time I would see him sitting there on the door step, I would call Carol's attention to him. She would look at him and scold, "Don't you dare! You know that you are not allowed in this house."

Meatball would sit there as the other cats pranced in and out going along on their merry way. He would just sit there and watch envying their privileges.

One day Meatball came up to the open back door and took up his observation post. Carol and I both looked at him and shrugged our shoulders. As we stared at him, he slowly lifted one paw and placed it slightly inside the kitchen door. We both jumped on him "Don't you dare," we demanded and he pulled the wayward paw back to his legitimate territory. Carol and I then turned our attentions back to our kitchen chores.

Suddenly Meatball exploded. Without warning he leaped across the kitchen threshold and made a mad hectic dash all around the kitchen. He was peddling so fast he was skidding and sliding all over the place. When he finished the kitchen he dove into the living room. He ran up and over everything. He made a complete circle then dashed back through the kitchen and out onto the back step. At which point he stopped, sat down in his usual longing position and stared up at us.

"Carol we've made that cat into a neurotic, a social reactionary, a deviant," I said.

A short time later Meatball disappeared. I have often wondered if he ever found a home where he was fully accepted.

Our world is full of Meatballs today and they are exploding everywhere. Some people make their own children into Meatballs. We've made the whole country of Mexico a Meatball nation. France has its own Meatballs. They were tipping over cars and setting them on fire not too long ago. Even Denmark has Meatballs and so does most of the European Community. England is full of Meatballs. For centuries the Irish were British Meatballs. India has always had its Meatballs and so has China and Asia. Russia has its Meatballs too. As I write, we have people all over Africa trying to wipe out all their Meatballs. Recently in Yugoslavia they had a Meatball cleansing going on. There are Meatballs everywhere and they are not happy. A Meatball knows when it is being treated like a Meatball. Even a dumb stray cat knows when it is being treated like a Meatball.

Oh how she will miss me

The other morning on the TV they had a special program dealing with the tragedy and heartbreak and personal loss of losing a dearly loved spouse after many years of faithful marriage. It seems that many a spouse actually devolves into a state of depression. They often lose their personal commitment to life. Some become so tragically morose, that they make themselves sick and often die not too long after their longtime companion has passed.

This made me think about my personal situation. My wife and I have been together now for over thirty years. We are exactly like the type of people being discussed in that study. We have been through the bad and the even worse; we have done with little and totally without; we have never been richer but we have often been poorer and we're still here - together, till death do us part.

The more I thought about that study the worse I felt. I could not stop thinking how terrible it is obviously going to be for my poor wife when I am no longer here. Oh my, how she is going to miss me when I'm gone. It makes me sick at heart to even think about it. I don't really know how she will be able to cope.

I can imagine her waking up at three o'clock in the morning because the automatic yard light went on - and it will actually be the yard light and not me looking for a book to read in the bedroom because I can't sleep.

Then the morning sun will finally be on the horizon. She will stumble out to the kitchen and when she passes the bathroom, that familiar odor that has always caused her to burst - "God Richard, was there something dead inside of you? Holy cow, light a match, spray something; think of the other people that come behind you." – will be but a sad reverie of days past.

Then she will step into the living room to turn on the TV and she will not have tripped over a pair of my snickers and dirty socks that would be in front of my big easy chair. She will sigh and mumble to herself, "I guess he is really gone."

She will go to the sink to get coffee water and there will be no cereal bowl with dried-on milk from my late night snack sitting there staring up at her. A small tear will drop from the corner of her eye.

When she goes to do the laundry there will be no wet, smelly towel sitting in the bottom of the bucket. Never again when she's cleaning up the yard or mowing the lawn will she be able to look over at the porch and see me there drinking a beer and reading my book. Who will she find to hold the other end of that 2x4 she needs to cut? I'm sure her heart will sink - if not break.

When she is talking with one of her sisters or a friend on the phone she will no longer be able to say, "Well, of course Richard doesn't agree with this but ..." When a battery clock or smoke detector stops or anything breaks or there is a new ding on the car door, there will be no Richard to accuse, it will have to be all her fault. This alone could make life very difficult for my poor beloved. She may not want to go on. (Excuse me while I blow my nose - this is really beginning to get to me.) How horrible this is all going to be for her.

When she wants to buy something at a department store she will just buy it and there will be no one there frowning and making her feel guilty for doing so. The checkbook will always be balanced and there will be no un-entered or misdated checks.

There will be no one to tell her that her mother didn't really know what the heck she was talking about, or that her father had a legitimate right to get drunk every now and then - as does her husband.

When I'm gone, life is truly going to be a sad experience for my poor darling. This is very sad. I have always told my wife that I was put here for her by God, so that she could stop thinking about herself. The burden of her happiness has been my burden and my goal in life.

Now what will she find that could ever replace me? Is there anything that could really replace me? I think that all of you out there know the answer to that question as well as I do.

152

She will be a ship without a sail or a rudder. She will be a soul lost in the darkness. Just thinking about how she will miss me when I'm gone is almost enough to make me weep. Her life will be like a Greek tragedy. When I am gone she will be so alone. She will be in such misery. She will have only her own thoughts to frustrate her. It will be so sad.

And there I'll be – up in heaven – counting my blessings and reaping my reward. Don't worry sweetheart, I'll put in a good word for you with "the Man" upstairs.

Unemployment and my depression mentality

A friend of mine just lost his job and went to Tallahassee and filed for unemployment. Even though he had worked steady for the last five years, he didn't qualify.

Less than 30% of those who lose their jobs in the State of Florida qualify for unemployment. On a national basis the figure is pretty much the same. A few states are better but most states are the same as Florida or worse.

The rules for collecting unemployment have been changing ever since the Reagan revolution in the 1980s. In most states you can no longer collect if you were fired, or let go, or you quit. The period of required working time has been extended. You can't collect if you have been working part time - even if you have been working 90 hours a week at 3 different part time jobs. The amount of the compensation checks has been cut and the length of time that you are allowed to collect has been cut. The current administration wants to lower (or already has) by 75% the employer's contribution to the fund and turn over the administration of the program entirely to the states. Staffing has already been cut to a minimum and retraining programs and finding jobs for people is secondary or nonexistent.

I have what is termed, sociologically, as a "Depression Mentality." I was not a "Depression baby," nor was I a child in the 30s. But my Mom and Dad were, and to add insult to injury in the late 40s and through the 50s my hometown suffered through Great Depression unemployment rates. During the 50s in my hometown unemployment was between 30 and 40 percent.

Many people in my old neighborhood didn't consider the 1929 Depression to be an accident. It was considered to be retribution against the workers by the powerful big business owners of the period. The 50s depression in our mill town was considered to be more of the same. The mill owners didn't want to pay the local workers so they shut down the mills and took their equipment and machines elsewhere. They left us the polluted waterways and the redbrick monster mill-buildings to clean up or dismantle. This is much the same as what is happening today. The industries and the explanations have changed but the tactics are the same.

But even though 4 out of every 10 workers were unemployed in my hometown, 6 out of every 10 still had a job. When I talk with many of my old friends about those times, only those whose fathers didn't have a job remember those days as hard times. And in reading about the Depression I find that the same obliviousness applied to the people of that era.

Franklin Delano Roosevelt actually hired newspaper photographers to go out and take pictures of soup kitchens and people sleeping in the streets and under bridges, and children living in squalor so that the Americans who still had their jobs could see and then believe the extent of the economic collapse. It seems that if the flame wasn't burning their fanny they couldn't see it. They needed pictures.

My Dad was one of those who worked most of his life in one of the mills. When he lost his job, he collected checks. Those checks were a life saver.

It is beginning to look to me that the good old unemployment check is on its way out – it has morphed into another "entitlement" as opposed to a benefit or right or a social responsibility.

It does seem that there are a lot of things that are now on their way out: college education for regular folks, retirement pensions, social security, health care, savings accounts, home owner's insurance, immigration, the bill of rights, free flu shots, low income housing, affordable drugs, good government jobs, mental health institutions, fathers, good paying jobs, American Industry, American exports, free public education, freedom from torture, a right to privacy and the sanctity of your home and your personal possessions, safe and honest banking, the volunteer army, the middle class, income tax, nursing homes, a skinny Oprah, a stable economy, local government, federal spending on anything but war and active duty personnel, aid to dependent children, racial tolerance,

155

religious tolerance, peace, security, a roof over one's head and hope for the future.

But being an optimist, I always turn to the positive. There are today more millionaires than ever before in American history, gated communities are growing in leaps and bounds, tummy tucks, liposuction and nonessential plastic surgery is booming and I have heard recently that an updated version of Queen for a Day is in the making.

For you young folks who never saw Queen for a Day, I think you guys will love it. This show would gather up all these desperate, poor, distraught, women - pregnant, husbandless, abused and battered. They would bring them out onto the stage to relate their tragic stories. The one with the worst, most degrading, humiliating, depressing story as determined by an applause meter would be crowned Queen for a Day. She would usually win a new washing machine, a stove or a refrigerator. Everyone watching at home would be in tears because they also needed new kitchen appliances. It was a wonderful show, and it looks like the times are coming where it will be considered wonderful once again. I can hardly wait. Let's all follow the bouncing ball and sing along! Happy days are here again ...

Buying a shower

For those of you who have never spent five or ten years living in a Chevy van under bridges, farmers' equipment shelters, in orange groves, apple orchards, grocery store parking lots, rest areas etc., this should be a new insight.

One big memory that both my wife and I still talk about today is stopping to buy a hot shower.

I'll bet you didn't know that you could buy a hot shower. Well, when we were on the road you could buy a hot shower at most any campground.

Bathing with a gallon jug of warm water, a sponge and a face cloth has its rewarding aspects, but after awhile the thought of a lingering hot shower becomes overpowering. To think of standing under a continuous flow of clean hot water and luxuriating, actually became a compulsion and periodically through our years on the road we had to give in and throw away a dollar each on that extravagance.

Never since our return to civilized living have I ever turned on our shower or our water tap at home without thinking of the wonder of it all. That little turn knob or lever on your sink or bath tub is not actually connected to God. And the fact that water comes spewing forth is not really a miracle. It takes a whole bunch of pipes and a whole system of people to make that experience the reality which is taken for granted by us all.

How many of us ever wonder where that water comes from and how it gets to our homes? When we first "homesteaded" our place here in Eastpoint, my brother-in-law and me pounded down both our water wells. We still have our well functioning. We use the water for the garden.

I can remember the guilt caused by my lingering at one of those $1.00 campground showers. I often thought the lady or fellow who sold me the shower would grab me on my way out and yell, "Do you realize that you used 150 gallons of hot water just now!" But it never happened.

We often got by on five one gallon containers of water per week in our travels. It takes five gallons of water just to flush the average house toilet one time. Your automatic clothes washer and dish washer are unbelievable in the number of gallons of water they consume. Carol and I once hauled every gallon of water that we used. I don't think that there are enough hours in a week for us to haul all the water we use today in our civilized existence.

As back-to-the-land-ers in Arkansas we got our drinking water from a mountain stream that ran through our property and we bathed in rain water that we caught in our canoe. We thought that we were doing great until we heard a warning on the radio about the danger of drinking water from a mountain stream. Pure mountain stream water is filled with chemicals and herbicides sprayed on the wilderness forests. Just because you live in the middle of a National Forest or wilderness area that doesn't mean your water is safe to drink. From then on we had to drive 20 miles once a week to a free artesian well in Mena, Arkansas for our water.

In some primitive campsites that we stayed at, water had to be hauled from a central location via a hand pump. When you have to walk to a well and then pump by hand every gallon and then haul it back to your home, you become very stingy in your use of water.

Here in Eastpoint my wife and I use 900 gallons of water per month each, but that is nothing compared to what most average city folks use today. The average person in the U.S. uses more than 3,000 gallons per month. Americans use 408 billion gallons a day. If we had to haul all that water from the pump in town to our homes I'll bet that 408 billion would shrink considerably. If we estimate the difference between what we actually need to live and what we use, to be waste - holy moley!

Today my wife and I really feel spoiled: we have indoor plumbing, we hop into the shower whenever we feel like it, and we have electricity - in every room! We even have an automatic dishwasher. I don't know whether to feel grateful, guilty, or privileged. I guess I should feel a whole bunch of each. In this respect one can truly say, God bless America!

Nothing lasts forever

I remember when I used to buy things thinking that they would last forever. It seems so silly today when I think of it. Where did I ever get such an idea? I remember in my not so distant past actually becoming annoyed if a screwdriver broke. Of course, screwdrivers are guaranteed today. You can buy a screwdriver and when you twist off the end of it trying to rotate a screw that is made out of stronger, harder metal than the screwdriver, you can bring the screwdriver back and they will give you another one that will do the very same thing. That's called a lifetime guarantee - you can spend your lifetime traveling back and forth to the hardware department at some department store. Actually our money has the same guarantee. If you don't think that it is worth anything you can bring it back to the bank and they will exchange it for more of the same.

I think I got this notion by being born too soon. We had the same refrigerator in my house from the beginning of my memories until I left home as an adult. My mother would save up the money to buy something once and then took care of it and it was understood to last forever. I had the same radio, the same bed, the same mattress, the same comforter, the same everything in my bedroom all my life at home.

Automobiles were like that too. Actually when Henry Ford manufactured his first Model T, it was advertised as so simple that even a "woman" could fix it. If the person who bought it couldn't fix it, no one in those days would have bought one. Today nobody can fix an automobile. If your automobile breaks even the dealership where you bought it probably can't fix it. And nobody buys a car for "keeps." Everything on today's automobile is designed to last as long as the warranty. In Cuba they are still driving the cars that were manufactured when I was growing up. They can be fixed and repaired forever.

Now I actually buy things just because it is time to get a new one. My old one still works but the company no longer makes parts for it and even if it did, there is no one who can remember how those parts used to fit together.

I buy clothes because that's what they have for sale, not because that is what I want. In my dressing career I've looked like Elvis, the Beach Boys, a guest on Hee Haw, a Wigger, and an off duty marine.

Sometimes I buy a new thing simply because they no longer sell supplies for my old thing.

Today I don't even expect that anything I buy will last. There are many things I buy to use just once and throw them away. I spend my disposable income buying disposable things. If anything I buy lasts longer than the warranty I feel I won.

I buy tape that doesn't stick to anything and glue that only sticks to my fingers and eyelids. I buy scissors that can't cut paper. I buy hammers that shatter pounding a nail. I buy light bulbs that fizzle out as I screw them in. I buy broken things that come in packaging that can't be opened with a blow torch. I buy knives that can cut through a tin can but won't slice a loaf of French bread. I buy T-shirts marked XX large that won't fit over my head and if they do get over my head they don't hang low enough to cover my belly button. I buy socks that form a hole in them as I put them on my feet for the first time. I buy hamburger and chicken livers that go bad while waiting for the frying pan to heat up. I buy chickens, ham and beef that lose weight just sitting on the counter. I buy vegetables that you can't even wash the salmonella from. I buy cans of tuna fish packed in water, that contain more water than tuna fish. I order things on the Internet that I know can't work. I guess that I have become so accustomed to being cheated that I have a longing for the feeling.

We don't even discuss "workmanship" anymore. The only place that I hear workmanship even being mentioned is on the Antique Road Show and This Old House.

My wife and I were watching a show about woodworking. My wife's grandfather was a carpenter and a house builder. "Do you think that your grandfather could have done that?" I asked.

160

"Yes," she replied, "but he would have done it with a hand saw and a rasp. In his day workmanship wasn't covering up sloppiness in an attempt to make it look professional. My grandfather used to do everyday of his life what the carpenter of today doesn't even believe is possible."

People go to college and don't specialize in anything. If they do, by the time they graduate their chosen specialty could very well be obsolete. Jobs are disappearing faster than you can learn how to do them. What you want to study today in college is flexibility and elasticity. You have to be flexible enough to do anything that is asked of you and then you've got to be able to stretch it out long enough to pay your rent or next mortgage payment.

Getting robbed

One thing that a business owner must think about that doesn't enter the mind of the average person is getting robbed. Having had experience in managing businesses for other people, I was aware of this problem when I opened my own local business. Eventually I had three cash registers in my little ice cream parlor each containing $150 in start up cash. I know that doesn't seem like much money but 450 bucks is a lot of money to some people. I won't mention all of what I did in my local business to protect myself, my wife and the little bit of money I accumulated daily because it was probably illegal.

The police and all the experts tell you that if anybody confronts you, don't resist - give them all your money and hope for the best. But after reading a number of stories about all the whackos out there, who rape, murderer and kill people just for the fun of it, I questioned all the authoritative advice. I had a small baseball bat under each cash register - along with other things - and I told my wife that I would be attacking anyone who tried to rob us. We had an attack plan. I felt that rather than being carted off in the trunk of some insane person's car, shot six times in the face and then dumped off the edge of a cliff, I would go out fighting. I am very happy to report that no one ever tried to rob us.

But I have a rather interesting recollection from my days as a restaurant manager in the "big" city.

I had been instructed by the company to make daily deposits each evening at the night deposit drop at the bank. But the local newspapers were full of stories about people getting robbed in just that way. On top of that on many occasions, I didn't shut down the restaurant until as late a two o'clock in the morning. It didn't seem wise to me to be pulling up to a night deposit box at two o'clock in the morning and strolling up to the box with five or six thousand dollars. I opted to hide the evening deposit in the floor safe and make my deposits during the day. Of course, this meant on a long weekend or on holidays when the banks were closed, I had a lot of money in my tiny floor safe back in the manager's office.

Things went fine for quite awhile. But then one evening I got a call at four or five in the morning. It was the police. They had been called by the security alarm people who gave them my number. They wanted me to come down to the restaurant as quickly as possible because they felt that they had a robber trapped inside the restaurant and they needed the man with the keys.

When I got there the place was surrounded - there were cruisers everywhere. The second I stepped out of my car, I had five guys all over me. I told them who I was and they brought me over to a plain clothed detective. He explained the situation to me. He wanted me to open the back door with my key, disable the alarm, and proceed as quickly as possible to the light switches. I was to snap on all the lights and the cops would take it from there.

I went over to the back door with the key. I turned off the security alarm. I opened the back door.

At this point the detective, or whatever he was, came up behind me quickly. He put one hand on my left shoulder and then stuck his revolver arm under my right arm pit.

"Okay, we're going in. As soon as we get in there I want you to go to the nearest light switch."

I started to move forward as he shoved me from behind, but then I stopped. I said, "No offense, sir, but it doesn't seem to me that the person with the gun should be standing behind me. Shouldn't you be in front of me?"

He said, "Yeah well, I don't know where the lights are and what if the guy in there is armed and starts shooting?"

I felt that was my line.

"That is a very good question," I said. "Shouldn't the man who has the training in dealing with this sort of behavior be going first?"

"Well, that's true and normally I would but I am retiring next week and I have seen too many of my buddies end their careers just like this. I've been looking forward to my retirement for a very long time and I am not about to screw it up now."

Naturally understanding the problems of professional working people and compassionate to their plight, I went forward in the dark with his gun arm projected from under my right armpit and his body protected behind my body. I rushed to the nearest light switch and flipped on the lights.

Just in case you are wondering, the bad guy was inside but he didn't shoot and I'm still alive. I do hope my friend the detective had a long enjoyable and healthy retirement.

Health, happiness, and a hot fudge banana split!

This petite, well dressed, shapely middle-aged woman stepped up to one of my ice cream cases. She scanned the varieties of ice cream like she was looking over a whole table of dead fish - blood, guts and everything. I had seen the type over and over.

Standing behind her is a red faced, jolly man, sporting a double chin and a good sized pot belly.

His designer wife hems and haws. She just can't make up her mind. Her decision is not perplexed because of all the different flavors being offered at Hobo's Ice Cream Parlor — now Hog Wild Bar-B-Q in Carrabelle. Her actual decision is whether she wants to go on starving and punishing herself or if she should indulge in the perversion and lust of ice cream.

"Do you have any sugar free ice cream?" she stumbles, hesitantly.

"Yes, I do. I have three different varieties."

"Do they taste good?" she peeps.

"I don't know. I don't eat that stuff," I tell her. "But people, who are diabetic or dying of some other incurable disease, tell me that it is pretty good."

The "Hey Norm" type guy standing behind her is still smiling but getting a little fidgety.

"Could I try a little taste of that one right there," she says pointing.

I get a plastic spoon and I proceed to get her a sample portion.

"Oh ... oh, you see that dab of strawberry lying there in the chocolate that I have chosen. Would you please remove that?"

I spoon out the dab of strawberry and also grab up a portion of the chocolate - just to make sure that I get it all."

As I remove the spoon from the tub of ice cream Norm says, "What are you going to do with that?"

"I'm going to throw it into the trash can," I tell him.

"No, no, no!" he says, shaking his head vigorously. I'll eat that." I pass him the spoon.

"Is it possible to get a half scoop, or do I have to get a whole scoop?" little miss Slim & Trim asks.

"Well, I will gladly give you as little as you want but the lowest price will be that of one full scoop."

The poor, troubled woman sighs deeply. "Okay, give me half a scoop of the sugar free chocolate."

"You want that on a homemade waffle cone or a regular cone?"

"Does the homemade cone have sugar in it?"

"Lady, everything in here has sugar in it except the sugar free ice cream that you ordered. And only god knows what that stuff has in it in place of the sugar. I'm sure some research scientist is injecting rats with it in some secret laboratory as we speak. Choose your own poison, lady."

"Can you put it in a cup?"

"Sure!"

"And what about you, sir?"

"Yeah, I want the largest banana split that you have. I want it filled with the richest chocolate ice cream you have but instead of the usual toppings I want it drenched in hot fudge and covered with a ton of whipped cream - and don't skimp on the nuts."

"No problem."

The little lady almost has a heart attack. She tish, tish, tishes and shakes her head in total disgust.

"Don't yell for me when you are rolling around on the floor clutching your chest. It is your life! You are a big boy now."

I look at Norm. He smiles.

"Don't forget, I like whipped cream. And could I get three maraschino cherries - one on each stack of ice cream."

"You know sweetheart, I just recently read in Eat Right and Never Die magazine that maraschino cherries don't digest in the human body."

"Well, what the heck happens to them?" asks Norm.

"They putrefy and then rot out your small intestine."

166

"I don't think I have a small intestine. Everything I have is big. So don't worry about it, honey."

"I'm not worried! Do I look worried? Your life insurance is all paid up."

"Honey, you will die of anorexia and I'll be living on an island in the South Pacific with a village of native beauties who all think that fat men are beautiful."

"We'll see."

"No Honey, unfortunately you won't - but I will!"

After Norm got his hot fudge banana split, they strolled out onto the little porch that looked out onto highway 98. She was snuggled up next to him and whispering into his ear. He was shaking his head negatively. Finally he said, "Oh all right! Go get another spoon."

When I next looked out at the couple she had tossed her sugar free in the trash can and they were each taking turns spooning into his giant, all chocolate, hot fudge banana split with lots of whipped cream and three maraschino cherries.

On their way out I said, "Well now with a little luck, you both might die simultaneously."

"Yeah, having sex I hope!" said he.

"Oh shut up!" said she.

Can't afford to die

All my life, I've had the same problem. No matter what it is, I just can't afford it.

The first bicycle that I wanted to buy cost $52 - I had $48. The first secondhand car that I wanted to buy cost $150 - I had $120. One year's tuition at the university was $3000 - I had $300. I wanted to buy my wife a nice wedding ring - she settled for a $30 plain gold band that we got at a flea market in Fort Lauderdale. It doesn't fit any more. She keeps it in a box in her dresser.

After my wife and I were married for awhile we went shopping for a home in Miami. We learned that even though we both had the best paying jobs in our lives we couldn't afford a home. We could have put a down payment on one, but it would have taken two lifetimes to pay for it. We would have been willing to live two lifetimes, but the option was not made available.

We ended up leaving Miami and our good jobs and began our adventure of Hobo-ing America. We lived in a van and slept under bridges and under equipment shelters all over America. We met bunches and bunches of people who could afford even less than what we could afford. In America we all know that there are no limits for those at the top, but unfortunately there is also no limit for those at the bottom.

We got our first home here in Eastpoint. We couldn't really afford it but we bought it anyway. It was a trailer home and it cost $8,886 new. We almost didn't get it paid for, but somehow we managed. As things stand today in Florida, I can't afford to insure it and I can't afford to sell it. It also seems that some people don't want me to live in it anymore. They say it isn't safe and that people like me aren't paying enough taxes. Unfortunately where they want me to go and live instead of living in my trailer is even less safe and I can't afford to do that either – and from what I understand it is a lot hotter.

I have just become eligible for Medicare. I can't afford it.

Now recently my wife and I have both reached the age where we have the opportunity to die. We have been analyzing our financial options and we have both come to the conclusion, that we can't afford it. If either of us dies, the other will not have adequate income to live on. The only way that we can both afford to die is if we can do it simultaneously. I've been thinking recently about that movie where those two women, Thelma and Louise, drive their car off the top of a cliff. At least they went out with a blaze of glory.

I guess, as people are prone to tell me these days, I should have done more planning. I should have gotten a 401K.

Well, most of my life there was no such thing. But I couldn't have afforded it anyway. And even if I could have I probably wouldn't have gotten one because I would have figured it was another scam. I would have figured that if I had saved all my life putting all my "extra" money into this 401K that by the time I became eligible to collect it, it would have disappeared. Like the pension programs at Ford Motor Co., or General Motors, or Colt Revolver Co., or Good Year Tire and so many others that are rapidly vanishing today. Somehow there would be an "equity" problem; there would be a "liquidity" imbalance. And like the Great Depression of 1929, or the S&L catastrophe of recent vintage, or the current mortgage crisis all the money would evaporate and, of course, there would be no one to blame. Everybody was just doing their job - business as usual. Yes it would be true that suddenly a few people would have billions and millions of people would suddenly have nothing, but...

I would probably have decided like most young people today, that I would take the gamble. I'll either strike it rich or I'll die broke.

I'm sure glad that I didn't have any children. Of course my wife and I realized that we couldn't really afford to have any children but most young people who really can't afford to have children do it anyway. Like Malthus once said and other conservatives say today, if poor people would just stop breeding, we would have no poverty.

I suppose.

In any case, since my wife and I have both figured that neither of us can afford to die, we have made a pact. I won't die as long as she won't die. It is going to be like The Survivor on the TV - stay tuned for next week's challenging episode.

ALSO BY
RICHARD EDWARD NOBLE

HOBO-ING AMERICA
A workingman's tour of the U.S.A.

A SUMMER WITH CHARLIE
A story about the last days of a young sailor

HONOR THY FATHER AND THY MOTHER
A tragic novel

A LITTLE SOMETHING
Poetry and Prose

www.ingramcontent.com/pod-product-compliance
Lightning Source LLC
LaVergne TN
LVHW011912080426
835508LV00007BA/496